10/98

Native American Biographies

Maria Tallchief

Native American Ballerina

Paul Lang

Enslow Publishers, Inc.

44 Fadem Road   PO Box 38
Box 699   Aldershot
Springfield, NJ 07081   Hants GU12 6BP
USA   UK

Library of Congress Cataloging-in-Publication Data

Lang, Paul, 1948–
    Maria Tallchief: Native American ballerina / Paul Lang.
       p. cm. — (Native American biographies)
    Includes bibliographical references (p.) and index.
    Summary: Tells the story of ballerina Maria Tallchief, focusing on
her Native American background and her rise to fame with the New
York City Ballet.
    ISBN 0-89490-866-9
    1. Tallchief, Maria—Juvenile literature. 2. Ballerinas— United States—
Biography—Juvenile literature. 3. Osage Indians —United States—
Biography—Juvenile literature. [1. Tallchief, Maria. 2. Ballet dancers.
3. Osage Indians—Biography. 4. Indians of North America—Biography.
5. Women—Biography.] I. Title. II. Series.
GV1785.T32L36   1997
792.8'092—dc21
[B]   96-52555
                                           CIP
                                           AC

Printed in the United States of America.

10 9 8 7 6 5 4 3 2 1

Photo Credits: Alfredo Valente, Boston Public Library Print
Department, Herald-Traveler Collection, p. 53; Archives & Manuscript
Division of the Oklahoma Historical Society, pp. 28, 108; Boston Public
Library Print Department, Herald-Traveler Collection, pp. 97, 99, 111;
Courtesy of the Boston Public Library, Print Department, p. 65; Erwin
Blumenfeld, New York Public Library for the Performing Arts, Dance
Collection, p. 89; Jonathan Tichenor, New York Public Library for the
Performing Arts Dance Collection, p. 7; Larry Colwell, New York Public
Library for the Performing Arts, Dance Collection, p. 42; New York
Public Library for the Performing Arts, Dance Collection, p. 48; Vincent
Dillon, Virgil Robbins Collection, Archives & Manuscript Division for the
Oklahoma Historical Society, pp. 13, 21, 30; Walter Owen, New York
Public Library for the Performing Arts, Dance Collection, pp. 74, 77.

Cover Photo: Dexter Press, New York Public Library for the Performing
Arts, Dance Collection

❊➤ CONTENTS ◄❊

MARIA TALLCHIEF AND THE FIREBIRD

There is a story that Maria Tallchief was so relaxed that she baked an apple pie just before opening night of *The Firebird*, the 1949 ballet that would make her famous. In fact, she recalls being "a nervous wreck" before the first performance, lying in her bed "shaking with terror."[1] Until that time, no ballerina born and trained in the United States had ever succeeded as the star of a major American ballet production. This version of *The Firebird* was the brainchild of George Balanchine, the great

Russian-born choreographer. (A choreographer is the person who designs and often directs ballets or other dances for the stage.)

Tallchief was trying to measure up to the demands of the role and the hopes of the ballet company in New York City. The company was relying on her to perform the most challenging dancing she had ever attempted. Those around her were amazed by the intensity with which she attacked the role. "The ballet was made for Maria," according to Francisco Moncion, Tallchief's dancing partner in the production, "and she went after it like a demon, with ferocity, as if possessed."[2]

❖New Beginnings❖

Maria Tallchief was twenty-four years old on opening night in 1949 and was far away from her birthplace on the Osage Indian Reservation in Fairfax, Oklahoma. Her parents had moved to California with Maria and her sister Marjorie when the girls were still children. While Tallchief's parents remained there, Maria and Marjorie moved on.

The weeks before the premiere were especially difficult. Tallchief attended rehearsals for *The Firebird*, and for the ballets of a touring company where she was soon to appear. George Balanchine and Tallchief had married three years before. The title role he had created for her in *The Firebird* contained some of his most brilliant—and difficult—steps.

— ❖ —

Maria Tallchief is shown here with her partner Francisco Moncion in Balanchine's The Firebird *(1949), set to the music of Igor Stravinsky.*

Tallchief had just one week to prepare for the role, and as if all this were not enough, she was recovering from a recent operation to remove her tonsils.

The Firebird had other famous and talented people connected with it apart from Tallchief and Balanchine. Igor Stravinsky, perhaps the most respected modern composer, had written the music for the ballet in 1910. He worked closely with Balanchine, adapting it for the new production. The brilliantly colored sets were designed by the artist Marc Chagall. He—like Balanchine, Stravinsky, and the story of the magical firebird itself—originally came from Russia.

◈ Crowd Pleaser ◈

From the moment on November 27, 1949, when Maria Tallchief first made her broad leap onto the stage, the New York City Center audience was spellbound. This exotic, passionate creature seemed to have flown into the spotlight from another world. Tallchief's body, according to one description, "was encased in flaming red as if it were her skin; her arms and shoulders glittered with gold dust. A long red feather sprang from her head and quivered in the air as she moved."[3]

Tallchief's lightning turns and jumps fascinated the first-night audience. Her final entrance in the ballet—revolving at almost super-human speed, her arms above her head gripping a flashing sword with both hands—was greeted with wild applause. When the final curtain fell, the audience rose to its feet and cheered so loudly, according to one spectator, "it was as if we were in a football stadium instead of a theater. . . . When Maria Tallchief took her first solo bow, I thought the roof would cave in. The applause went on and on. . . ."[4]

No audience in New York had ever before shown a home-grown ballet company such an enthusiastic reception. Maria Tallchief had struggled through years of hard work, occasional illness, and frequent discouragement. Now she was creating the dazzling centerpiece of an artistic and financial sensation that would bring American audiences flocking to the production. *"The Firebird* may well have been the ballet that made the New York City Ballet," according to one writer, and Maria Tallchief's performance was, in large part, the dancing that made *The Firebird*.[5]

THE OSAGE PEOPLE

Elizabeth ("Betty") Marie Tall Chief was born on January 24, 1925, in Fairfax, Oklahoma, to Ruth Porter Tall Chief and Alexander Tall Chief. The Tall Chiefs had three children together— Gerald, Betty Marie, and Marjorie. They shared their home in Fairfax with Alexander's mother Elizabeth ("Eliza") Bigheart, who retained the last name of her original family after marrying Alexander's father.

◈Native American Ancestory◈

Betty Marie's grandmother Eliza, like her grandfather, was a full-blooded member of the

Osage tribe. Betty Marie's mother, like Alexander's first wife who had died, was of European descent. She was Irish, Scottish, and German. The Tall Chief children were raised for the most part in Los Angeles—far away from the Osage Reservation, but they were proud of their Native American heritage.

Grandmother Eliza still wore traditional Osage clothes and had carried Betty Marie's father on her back, like a papoose. It was Grandmother Eliza who introduced Betty Marie to her Native American heritage. She told Betty Marie about the history, folktales, music, and dances of the Osage people.

From a very early age, Betty Marie became familiar with the look of the ceremonial dancers. She saw their brilliant special leggings, brightly colored shirts, beribboned breech cloths, and striking "roaches"—stand-up decorations of deer fur or porcupine quills. Sometimes a single eagle feather covered the back of their heads. The dancers also had their faces painted in a traditional design. They sang as the gourd rattles sounded, the bells that they shook tinkled, and the whistles made of eagle bones filled the air.[1] Betty Marie's training was in ballet and classical piano. She knew, however, the sounds and sights of ceremonies that had been performed by the Osage for generations. She would take pride in her Native American heritage all her life.

Betty Marie had a good reason to be proud of this heritage. Ancestors on her father's side had played

— ◈ —

Osage dancers are shown in traditional costume at the Gray Horse Dance Hall in Oklahoma early in the twentieth century.

crucial roles in the history of the Osage in the late nineteenth and early twentieth centuries.

In 1822 the Osage were forced to give up nearly all of their land claims to make way for white settlers. All they were left with was a reservation covering just over six thousand square miles in present-day southern Kansas.

In 1870 they were moved further south into a reservation in what is now northern Oklahoma. James Bigheart, the great-great-grandfather of Betty Marie Tall Chief, signed that treaty and also helped to write a tribal constitution in 1881. His son, Betty Marie's grandfather Peter Bigheart, was instrumental in negotiating a 1906 agreement that made mineral rights found under Osage land common property of the whole tribe. This led to a period of great prosperity for the Osage in the early decades of the twentieth century, after rich oil deposits were found on the land.

Osage history was not just a vague idea in the Tall Chief household. That history was made, in part, by Betty Marie's own relatives. Through her father and grandmother, Betty Marie could hear about these figures, not just as legendary leaders of the Osage, but as real people.

❖The History of the Osage to 1880❖

The Osage believe that they originally came down from the stars to populate the earth. "They floated down, landing in a red oak tree," according to the story, and as they fell, "their legs were stretched to grasp the limbs, and their arms were uplifted like the wings of an alighting golden eagle."[2] The Osage still perform a creation dance, with arms stretched to the sky like wings. The dance recalls the landing of the Sky People.

These "Sky People" found that "Land People" were already living on earth and soon the two peoples joined into one tribe, "Children of the Middle Waters," perhaps a reference to their early home on the banks of the Osage River, located in present-day western Missouri. Modern-day Osage can still trace their origins back to either the Sky People or the Land People clans (or divisions). To the Osage, the Middle Waters represented three of the four elements— water, land, and sky. According to the Osage, the Sky People descended to earth, and the elements were separated to form the world by *Wah'Kon-Tah*, the mysterious force controlling the universe.

Tribal affairs in the earliest times, and even into the nineteenth century, were controlled largely by tribal chieftains and by the "Little Old Men." These Little Old Men were seasoned older warriors who decided when the tribe would go to war or make peace. They set the standards of behavior for individual Osage. They were also responsible for the regular rituals and ceremonies that kept the tribe within the protection of *Wah'Kon-Tah*.

John Joseph Mathews was an Osage and a graduate of Oxford University in England. He described the role in legendary times of the Little Old Men in his epic history of his people, *The Osages: Children of the Middle Waters,* in 1961:

> *Each day the Little Old Men would rise and slowly draw their buffalo robes about them, singing their Rising Song, and say among themselves that they had now learned the will of Wah'Kon-Tah, and they would ask him to help them attain the order which he himself maintained in the sky. They would make certain songs and dances and create recitations for ritualistic use, so that Wah'Kon-Tah, the creator of order, could understand them and their desires and aid them in prolonging life through [plenty of] food and the bravery of their warriors.*[3]

❖Contact With Europeans❖

The Osage first encountered Europeans at the end of the seventeenth century. This was a few years after Jacques Marquette and Louis Jolliet of France had claimed all of the Mississippi Valley for France. Some time before the beginning of the eighteenth century, the rival Iroquois tribe drove the Osage from their lands in Virginia. The Osage followed game and water routes west of the Mississippi River into present-day northern Arkansas and western Missouri. Europeans who encountered the Osage in the late 1600s found them living in five permanent villages located on branches of the Missouri River in southwest Missouri.

French traders found the Osage to be excellent partners in business. They traded horses, metal utensils, guns, blankets, alcohol, and other European novelties in exchange for furs. The Osage allied with the French against the Chickasaws and other tribes who allied with the English. Osage warriors sometimes took members of other tribes as slaves to exchange with the French for manufactured goods.

France's North American colonial empire, built on the fur trade, ended with the Treaty of Paris in 1763. In 1803, fourteen years after George Washington took office, President Thomas Jefferson paid France $15 million for the Louisiana Purchase. This was a vast territory stretching east to west from the Mississippi River to the Rocky Mountains, and north from the border with Canada to the Gulf of Mexico to the south. This roughly doubled the area of the United States.

❖The Nineteenth Century❖

The history of the Osage in the nineteenth century is best understood when we consider how powerless they really were against the full might of the American government at that time. Native American tribes throughout the country found, to their dismay, that the American government was happy to make treaties ensuring tribes "eternal" rights to at least some of their traditional lands. Unfortunately, these treaties would routinely be broken when white settlers and their representatives in Washington, D.C., applied enough pressure. The government was quick to put down any resistance to the new terms forced onto the tribes by using whatever armed pressure was necessary.

Native Americans saw their land not as something to be bought or sold, but as a sacred trust to be preserved for their children and their children's children. For this reason, many tribes resisted the very idea of treaties that gave away the territory where their ancestors had hunted and lived. Tribes that refused to negotiate treaties, however, risked forced removal at gunpoint from the lands or even slaughter.

❖Signing Treaties❖

For most of the early nineteenth century, the Osage would see much of their hunting territory invaded by other tribes. They were forced from their land by ever-increasing white settlement east of the Mississippi. In 1808–1809 the Osage were forced to sign a treaty with the United States government. It gave up their claims to much of their territory—about two hundred square miles—in exchange for a yearly payment of fifteen hundred dollars. This money was used to pay off whites who had made claims against the tribe. It was also used for tools, farming, and gun repair. The Osage were pushed farther west to present-day Kansas. They reluctantly signed a second treaty with the United States government in 1825. They were forced to give up what lands remained to them in what is now Kansas, Missouri, Arkansas, and Oklahoma (45 million acres). All that remained for them was a reservation 50 miles wide and 125 miles long in Kansas. From 1808 to 1825 the Osage gave up almost 100,000,000 acres in exchange for about $166,000 in cash, animals, and agricultural equipment. This was just one penny for every six acres of land.[4]

Washington Irving, the author of *The Legend of Sleepy Hollow* and *Rip Van Winkle*, joined an expedition to the territories west of Arkansas in 1832. By this time thousands of Native Americans, including the Osage, had been forcibly removed to the prairies of the Midwest. Irving gave a detailed account of Osage life as it was then, including accounts of buffalo warriors, war parties, and tribal chants and dances. He found the Osage men "stately fellows; stern and simple in [dress] and aspect." He further noted that they "wore no ornaments; their dress consisted merely of blankets, leggings, and moccasins. Their heads were bare; their hair cropped close, excepting a bristling ridge on the top, like the crest of a helmet, with a long scalp lock hanging behind."[5]

Two years later, in 1834, American artist George Catlin sketched and painted a number of Osage. He noted how much they had retained their traditional ways despite contact with whites: "Though living near the borders of the civilized community, they have studiously rejected every civilized custom. They are dressed in skins of their own making . . . [except that they use] blankets instead of buffalo robes, which are now getting scarce among them."[6]

Catlin also observed how much disease and forced relocations had weakened the tribe. Until recently, he wrote:

> The Osages were . . . a powerful and warlike tribe. They carried their arms fearlessly through all these realms. . . . Now the case is quite different. They have been repeatedly moved and jostled . . . [and] small-pox has taken its share of them two or three different times.[7]

The Osage came under pressure from both United States government agents and missionaries throughout the nineteenth century to "leave the blanket." They were pressured to abandon Native American speech, dress, and customs and become like whites—preferably taking up farming on the prairie land. The Osage had been forced into the Kansas Territory in the 1820s. Pro-slavery and anti-slavery forces often came into bloody conflict there, even before the Civil War began in 1861.

◆The Civil War◆

The Civil War pitted the Union of northern states against the Confederacy of southern states. In the first year of the war some of the Osage signed a treaty with the Confederate forces. The Osage offered to allow the Confederate soldiers to use waterways through Osage land and to give up small plots of land

— ◆ —

The Osage were forced to move west many times in their history. Here an Osage is shown watering his horses on the bank of the Arkansas River.

where Confederate forts could be located. In exchange, they received a promise (earlier made and broken in treaties with the United States government) that the Osage would "have exclusive and undisturbed possession [of their land] during all time, as long as the grass shall grow and water run."[8] The Confederacy had neither the ability nor the intention of ever enforcing the terms of the treaty.

Eventually, different parts of the tribe allied themselves with the Union or Confederate causes. Some Osage were pressured to support the war efforts of both sides. In fact, outbreaks of smallpox and measles were more immediate problems for most of the tribe during the Civil War years. In 1863, however, the Osage had to defend themselves against recruiting officers of the Confederate Army when a tribe member was shot and killed on Osage territory. The Confederate soldiers were soundly defeated.

Toward the end of the Civil War, in 1865, the Osage provided a sort of "buffer zone" (neutral territory) between the two warring sides. The Osage faced occasional mistreatment from both armies. With the end of the war, whites in Kansas pressured the federal government to resettle Native Americans farther south.

One illegal squatter on Osage land in Kansas had a strong prejudice against Native Americans. He wrote his congressman in 1870:

> [H]urry up the removal of these lazy, dirty
> vagabonds. . . . It is folly to talk longer of a handful

of wandering savages holding possession of land so fair and rich as this. We want this land to make homes. Let us have it.[9]

The Osage were forced to sign another treaty with the United States government in 1870. The Osage were removed from Kansas and forced to settle in Indian Territory (present-day Oklahoma). The forced removal of the Osage was a severe blow to the tribe. It moved them from the rich game-filled land in Kansas to the rocky and more barren land of Indian Territory.

Famous Ancestors, Osage Wealth, and Childhood

James Bigheart, the great-great-grandfather of Betty Marie Tall Chief, had signed the 1870 relocation treaty. He was one of the first Osage to build a home on the new reservation in Indian Territory. Bigheart had been educated at a mission school. He achieved the rank of lieutenant fighting for the Union (northern) Army during the Civil War. He also spoke four Native American languages in addition to English and French. He was a full-blooded Osage chief who worked as interpreter and clerk for the Osage Agency (the United States government agency responsible for Osage affairs).

❖Betty Marie's Famous Ancestors❖

In 1881 at an Osage grand council meeting, James Bigheart was chosen to preside over the writing of a constitution for the tribe. The constitution created a National Council, headed by a principal and an assistant chief. The council would be responsible for interpreting treaties, collecting taxes, and settling arguments between tribal members. It also provided formal elections of officials. The first elections were held in 1882, but the Osage National Council only lasted until 1900. At that time the United States government forced the abolition (end) of the constitution. This put tribal control back under the United States government.

After constant pressure from white "Indian commissioners," politicians, and other whites who were hungry for even more land, the Osage were forced by the United States government in 1906 to abandon the idea of the whole tribe owning land as a community. They were forced to divide their reservation into so-called "allotments." James Bigheart's son Peter was the grandfather of Betty Marie Tall Chief's father Alexander. Peter played a crucial role in demanding an exception to the dividing of the land. With other full-blooded Osage he fought for the right to keep any profits from gas and oil that might be found under the ground as community property for the whole tribe.

❖Osage Wealth❖

This "underground" exception was eventually accepted by members of the tribe and it changed the future history of the Osage completely. The Osage were already the wealthiest Native American tribe (mostly from leasing land for grazing) when oil had first been discovered in 1894. At this time rich gas deposits were also found. If the oil and gas royalty wealth had been given only to those Osage under whose land the deposits were found, the tribe as a whole would not have been able to benefit from the wealth. As it turned out, however, during the first half of the twentieth century, the Osage tribe as a whole received $300,000,000 from gas and oil royalties. This was divided among about two thousand tribal members, giving the Osage the largest individual incomes of any nation in the world.[1]

The first twenty-five years of the twentieth century were a time of almost dizzying change for the newly-wealthy Osage. Newspapers were filled with amazing—and sometimes amusing—stories. They told of expensive limousines parked unused by Osage who had bought the cars without knowing how to drive them, newly-built homes furnished in the most extravagant and expensive way, and adults and children alike sporting gold jewelry. Stores in the

— ❖ —

Maria Tallchief's ancestors were important figures in Osage history, especially important in their tribe's contact with United States government officials. This Osage Indian Council posed for the camera in 1925, the year Maria Tallchief was born.

area regularly charged the Osage many times the normal price for goods.

Some whites saw a chance for easy money and proceeded to trick members of the tribe. Some whites cheated the Osage out of their royalty checks with get-rich-quick schemes and highly questionable "guardian" relationships to individual Osage. In one exceptional and sensational instance, a white man actually married an Osage woman and then had over twenty members of her family murdered so he could inherit their royalty rights.[2] Many tribal members, however, used their royalty money shrewdly. Some made sound investments and started businesses.

Osage purchases of bonds and contributions to the Red Cross during World War I (American participation 1917–1919) also greatly helped the war effort. The year 1925 was the high point for royalty money. Per-person payouts for that year were $13,200—the equivalent of over one hundred thousand dollars today.[3]

❖ Childhood in Fairfax, Oklahoma ❖

"The era of long black limousines was before I was born," Betty Marie Tall Chief remembered when she was twenty-nine years old. She explained, "We had no great wealth or splendor, but we had no hunger either."[4]

Betty Marie lived the first eight years of her life in Fairfax, Oklahoma, with her mother, father, older

— ❖ —

Dance has always been and continues to be an important part of Osage culture. This photograph of a crowded scene of Osage spectators and dancers was taken south of Fairfax, Oklahoma, Maria Tallchief's birthplace earlier in the century.

brother, Gerald, younger sister, Marjorie, and her father's mother, Eliza. Betty Marie's family did not live, as she later put it, in "wealth or splendor," but the local movie theater and pool hall were owned by her father.

Alexander Tall Chief enjoyed outdoor sports such as horseback riding. He was also an avid golfer. Betty Marie's mother, Ruth Porter Tall Chief, was at the center of Fairfax society. She did charity work with the church, played bridge, and gardened. Mrs. Tall Chief was particularly interested in all things involving the arts, especially music and dancing.

At three years old, Betty Marie was already sounding out simple melodies on the family piano. She also had the rare gift of being able to identify what note was being played just by hearing it. This is an unusual natural ability called "perfect pitch." Her mother recognized her daughter's talent and started her with piano lessons at age three. A year later Betty Marie began dancing lessons with a Tulsa, Oklahoma, teacher who visited Fairfax twice a week.

Betty Marie's brother Gerald, three years older than she, began violin lessons. He realized early, however, that his interests lay more with riding, working with horses, and playing sports. Younger sister Marjorie also showed great ability early. In fact, Marjorie would grow up to be a professional ballet dancer and teacher.

Even as children, however, the two girls were very different. Marjorie was like her father, and Betty Marie was more like her mother. Still the sisters were very close. They were sometimes even taken for twins. This was something that was easy to do since their mother dressed them in matching clothes.

Betty Marie looked forward to her dancing lessons much more than her piano lessons. Her mother, however, felt that her elder daughter could, with time and the proper training, become a concert pianist. Betty Marie was just five years old when she performed a solo dance to John Philip Sousa's rousing and patriotic "The Stars and Stripes Forever." She filled the stage with high-speed twirls. Betty Marie wore a small cape that, in a sensational finish, she unfurled to reveal an American flag. She waved it with amazing energy and grace.

Betty Marie and Marjorie were soon asked to perform at school and charity benefits. As Betty Marie remembered, "We loved it . . . and were willing to dance at anything from mothers' teas to rodeo—wherever they wanted entertainment, we were ready!"[5]

❖Moving to California❖

When Betty Marie was eight years old, her mother and father made a decision that changed the family's life forever. Fairfax, Oklahoma, simply did not have the piano or dance teachers from whom Betty Marie and Marjorie could benefit. Ruth Porter Tall Chief had a busy social life in Oklahoma, and Alexander Tall Chief loved working outdoors on his farm. Yet the family pulled up stakes and moved to Beverly Hills, California, in 1933. They were most likely escaping the poor economic conditions of the time and searching for a less isolated upbringing and a better education for the girls.

Maria Tallchief was asked in the 1990s what her favorite words were. In addition to grace and elegance, words one might expect from a great ballerina, the other words were all connected with her family. "My mother was a lady of great 'courage' and 'perseverance' [determination, refusal to give up] . . . My father had a wonderful sense of 'humor' (as did my grandmother Tall Chief)."[6]

The humor from her father's side of the family, along with a lifelong feeling of pride in her Native American heritage, would always stay with Tallchief. It would help her as she faced the challenges of a new home, new friends, and new teachers in California. She would also need all of her mother's courage and perseverance to carry her to the very top of the ballet world and make her the most famous and respected ballerina of her generation.

EARLY
TRAINING

The changes from the Osage reservation life in Oklahoma to the world of suburban Beverly Hills and nearby Los Angeles, California, were enormous for the Tall Chiefs. Native Americans were a novelty in well-to-do Beverly Hills, and other children at Betty Marie's elementary school greeted the new student with the war whoops they had learned from movies and by playing cowboys and Indians. "Why wasn't she wearing 'Indian' clothes?" "Did she paint her face like the Indians in the movies?" "Did her father have any scalps from fighting when he was younger?" they asked.

Betty Marie did not always know how to answer all of the questions she was asked. Gradually, however, she began to fit in with her new classmates. She excelled in writing original stories with clever plots and ingenious clues. She often took center stage in the classroom to recite her compositions.

❖Dance Lessons❖

Even more important for her future was the fact that she started taking dance lessons with a respected teacher named Ernest Belcher. Betty Marie had been dancing on her toes for years when she started her lessons with Belcher. She knew nothing, however, about the basic five positions that beginning ballet students first learn. Belcher realized that his promising young student needed to start at "step one." Betty Marie would have to forget everything she had been taught about toe-dancing and start to master the elementary exercises of ballet. This involved hours of difficult, and to many students, tedious practice at the waist-high horizontal bar (called by the French word *barre*) that is attached to the walls of a ballet studio.

For Betty Marie, these hours at the bar were not tedious. She even convinced her parents to put a bar in their house so she could practice at home. Just before she was twelve, she gave her first public performance since she had moved from Oklahoma. This was a vigorous display, arranged by Belcher, in "Indian" dress with her sister Marjorie at their public school and another with members of the Los Angeles Civic Opera Company.

At the insistence of Mrs. Tall Chief, Betty Marie continued to study classical piano. On January 24, 1937, when she turned twelve years old, she was the pianist in Frederic Chopin's first piano concerto. She also gave a dance recital to complete the program. A picture taken of her at this recital shows her seated at the piano wearing a ballgown of a sheer yellow material. She was surrounded by baskets of flowers and had blossoms around her neck and in her hair. She was "a slim, dark child with big eyes, a hesitant smile, and little pointed elbows . . . ."[1]

❖Madame Nijinska❖

In 1937, almost two years before Betty Marie started high school in Beverly Hills, Belcher introduced her to one of the most respected figures in the dance world, Bronislava Nijinska. Classes with Nijinska finally convinced Betty Marie's mother that the teenager should stop trying to master both piano and ballet. Betty Marie would concentrate only on dance. This ended a conflict between mother and daughter that had lasted for many years. Betty Marie was now free to pursue her first love. As her biographer Olga Maynard put it, "At seventeen Tallchief closed the lid of her piano forever on her projected concert career."[2]

Bronislava Nijinska was in her late forties when she opened a dance school in Los Angeles. Bronislava was the sister of the legendary Russian dancer Vaslav Nijinsky (1890–1950). Like her brother, she had been trained at the Imperial Ballet School in St. Petersburg, Russia. She and Vaslav had both danced in the innovative and highly acclaimed ballet company founded by Sergei Diaghilev in 1911. Her brother succumbed to mental illness in 1917 and had to stop his career. She, however, continued to dance.

In the early 1920s Nijinska became principal choreographer of the Diaghilev company. She also started her own company in 1932. Madame (French for Mrs.) Nijinska continued to choreograph ballets in Europe and South America after her company disbanded. Eventually she opened her ballet school in Los Angeles. She began teaching American students what she had learned during her long and distinguished dancing career.

Betty Marie had worked tirelessly to master many of the fundamentals that a young ballet dancer must know. With Madame Nijinska, she learned how the fundamentals could be used to create a theatrical presence. She also learned how the body could be used with the music to create emotional and artistic effects. Betty Marie learned early that there was no nonsense in Madame Nijinska's classes. This may

MT3

- Born in Fairfax, Oklahoma on a reservation

- Osage Indian

have suited the young dancer's own serious, no-nonsense attitude. According to one description:

> When Nijinska's pupils walked into class, it was as if they walked onto the stage, and they had to stand or move as if in front of an audience. . . . If Maria had a sprain or a bruise she was not allowed to give way to it in class, but expected to dance full out. If she felt unable to do this she was to stay away . . . "Give your full attention to what you are doing," Nijinska told them, "or don't do it at all."[3]

❖David Lichine❖

Betty Marie and Marjorie also began to take classes with another famous choreographer, David Lichine. His wife Tatiana ("Tanya") Riabouchinska was a respected prima (star) ballerina. The Tall Chief girls were in awe of David Lichine. He was a demanding and sometimes strict teacher, but he was quite capable. His wife was a reassuring presence and called "Darling Tanya" by the girls.[4]

Madame Nijinska had created a ballet, *Chopin Concerto*, set to the same piece of music that Betty Marie had played in concert at age twelve. The choreographer began to make plans to introduce her promising fifteen-year-old student. Betty Marie was now a sophomore in high school. She was a principal soloist in a production of the *Chopin Concerto* at the huge Hollywood Bowl. Her sister Marjorie was also included as a dancer.

After this night, Betty Marie would understand the wisdom of Madame Nijinska's demanding attitude during her classes. She insisted that dancers perform "full out" even when their bodies started to fail them. During her performance, Betty Marie lost her footing and fell to the stage. This was a humiliating event, before an enormous crowd in her first important dancing role. She continued dancing, however, as she had been taught to do in class. Not only did Madame Nijinska comfort her, but reviews the next day kindly left out any mention of her misstep and even said she had showed a lot of spirit in her dancing.[5] After this performance, she later remembered, "I realized I didn't care a bit about sitting planted at the piano—and I love ballet. I like to be active and moving."[6]

◈Light Opera◈

During the next two years Betty Marie continued going to high school and taking dance classes. She even appeared with Marjorie as part of a light opera company in Los Angeles. Light opera companies usually sing in English and perform operettas, an early kind of musical comedy, rather than operatic epics by Richard Wagner, or grand operas by Mozart and Verdi. The director of the Ballet Russe de Monte Carlo, Serge Denham, offered to let her join his company. She could be a dancer-in-training if she would pay her own expenses. Mrs. Tall Chief was pleased that the director of an important dance company saw the talent of her daughter. She was insistent, however, that Betty Marie graduate from high school before starting a professional career.[7]

Betty Marie's professional career started small. During the summer after graduation, in 1943, she appeared as one of the background dancers in a ballet sequence in a Judy Garland movie called *Presenting Lily Mars*. Her father remarked humorously that Betty Marie was the first Osage to go out and earn her own living.[8]

❖To New York❖

Betty Marie Tall Chief had obeyed her mother and stayed in high school to graduate. Then plans were made for her to enroll in the University of California at Los Angeles. However, Madame Nijinska, David Lichine, and his wife, Tanya Riabouchinska, were all leaving for work in New York at this time. So Tall Chief's mother agreed to send her to New York, at least for a short time. Mrs. Tall Chief may have seen this as a vacation treat for Betty Marie before starting college. Her daughter would also be able to see if Serge Denham's offer to let her train with his Ballet Russe still held.

Betty Marie Tall Chief spent her first night in New York City sleeping on David Lichine's livingroom couch. She found it impossible at first to get past the front desk in Serge Denham's office. Gradually,

— ❖ —

Maria Tallchief is shown here supported by André Eglevsky. Melissa Hayden is also shown in Balanchine's Pas de Trois (Dance for Three), *which premiered in London in 1948.*

through Madame Nijinska and Tanya Riabouchinska, she was introduced to many dancers and teachers living in New York. She was encouraged to keep trying to audition for Serge Denham.

These must have been difficult days for Tall Chief. She was far from her family, separated from her parents and sister for the first time. She was discouraged at not even getting to reintroduce herself to the man most likely to give her a chance to prove herself as a dancer. To make matters worse, Tall Chief's mother still expected her to return to Los Angeles soon in order to start college there in the fall.

It would take almost a week of daily telephone calls to Serge Denham's office for Tall Chief to get an audition with the Ballet Russe, but she refused to give up. Mrs. Tall Chief had passed on her perseverance to her elder daughter. Now, in 1942, that perseverance would start to pay off. Betty Marie Tall Chief was about to become a full-time ballet dancer with company that had a world-wide reputation. She was about to take a new name, too—Maria Tallchief.

Touring with the Ballet Russe

Betty Marie Tall Chief might not have been able to join the Ballet Russe de Monte Carlo in 1942 if the United States had not recently entered World War II. Sol Hurok was the organizer and manager ("impresario") of the company. He, not Serge Denham, had the final say about hiring dancers. At this time he was only interested in taking on Europeans, mostly French and Russian dancers. However, with the war on, Europeans working in America were having trouble getting visas to leave the United States. Visas were essential since the tour of the Ballet Russe included several stops in Canada.

❖The First Tour and a New Name❖

Betty Marie Tall Chief finally got her audition with the Ballet Russe. While she waited to hear from the touring company, she started taking lessons at the School of American Ballet in New York City. The director, George Balanchine, would eventually become her husband. It was in his productions she would gain her greatest fame, but the Ballet Russe came first.

Serge Denham hired Tall Chief to join the company for its upcoming Canadian tour. Tall Chief was promised a permanent position as a dancer with the company and a "bonus" (not a regular salary) at the end of the tour. All of this would come, only if her work proved satisfactory, however.

The company's first performance on the tour took place in Ottawa, Canada. The ballet was called *Gaîeté Parisienne* ("Parisian merriment" or "Parisian frolic"). Tall Chief had a small part that called for a series of *fouettés*. These are quick revolutions in which the dancer supports herself on one leg while "whipping" the other, bent leg in a rapid in-and-out motion. The supporting leg must be precisely timed to alternate low and high positions in exact coordination with the "whipping" leg. Both movements had to be timed precisely with the lightning twirls that are required to make a perfect series of *fouettés*.

Tall Chief's reviews were excellent. One Canadian critic called her *fouettés* "ravishing" and "perfect," and added that she executed them with "shattering, electric effect."[1] Tall Chief may not have been totally pleased with her performance, though. She humbly wrote home: "There were no complaints, so I guess I did O.K."[2]

❖Summer Tour❖

During the summer tour Tall Chief learned new roles during exhausting rehearsals. Sometimes she doubled parts when needed. With time she was given more solos to perform. Other members of the company, both seasoned veterans of many years and aspiring young dancers, were not always kind to her. She began to feel a distinct unfriendliness from some of the other dancers. There were those who made her feel as though she were not really one of them. They made her feel as though she did not deserve the solo parts that were starting to come her way. Perhaps they were jealous of her talent. Sometimes she served as a replacement for dancers who were unable to go on at a given performance.[3] Some of the girls teased her about her serious manner. They called her "Princess Iceberg," or adding a slap at Tall Chief's heritage, a "wooden Indian."

Ruth Porter Tall Chief continued sending her daughter traveler's checks throughout the tour. Most of the company rode in inexpensive seats in the coach cars of the trains that carried them from city to city. Betty Marie Tall Chief was able to afford a sleeping car, like the principal dancers of the company.

— ❖ —

Maria Tallchief, as part of the corps de ballet of Gaîeté Parisienne, *performed with the Ballet Russe on their 1942 tour.*

This also caused resentment among some of the other dancers. When Tall Chief realized this, she joined the other members of the *corps de ballet* (dancers in the "background" who support the soloists) in coach.[4]

Her letters home continued to reflect her discomfort at not "fitting in" with the other dancers. In one, she wrote, "You cannot know what it is like to be the newest one in a ballet company. But I am learning. . . . Don't worry. I'll survive, no doubt. What matters is that I am dancing."[5]

Despite the emotional ordeals of the Ballet Russe tour, Betty Marie Tall Chief took full advantage of the opportunities it provided. She mastered new roles quickly and showed technical skill and artistry when allowed to step out of the *corps de ballet.*

The last train ride of the tour finally brought her back to New York City. The Ballet Russe offered her a contract for the coming season in New York. She would be a member of the *corps de ballet.* It would not be easy, she knew, to work her way back up to solo roles now that the company's European-born dancers were once again available to perform. She accepted the offer immediately, however.

◆ A New Name ◆

In 1942 Betty Marie Tall Chief was asked to take on a name that would sound more theatrical. All of the most famous ballerinas performing in America had been born and trained in Europe, many in Russia. By coincidence, when Tall Chief was made into one word, *Tallchief*, the last letters resembled the distinctive *"ieff"* ending of many Russian names. (Not many Americans would realize that the correct form for a woman's name in Russian would be "Tallchieva.") When preceded by a version—*Maria*—of her own middle name, *Tallchief* had just the right dramatic and foreign ring. The Ballet Russe would open its New York season with *Gaîeté Parisienne*. This was the ballet in which she had won such wonderful reviews in Canada. She had a small part in the *corps de ballet*. For the first time she used her new name, "Maria Tallchief," in the program. Soon even her parents and sister would use this new spelling of their last name.

◈Choreography by Madame Nijinska◈

Maria Tallchief was presented with an opportunity in the spring of 1943. One of the prima ballerinas hurt her foot and was unable to dance in *Chopin Concerto*. This was the ballet that Madame Nijinska had created and in which Tallchief had danced at the Hollywood Bowl and later on the Canadian tour.

Tallchief continued lessons with Madame Nijinska in New York after returning from Canada. Her trusted teacher encouraged her to practice the starring part in the *Chopin Concerto*. This way she would be outstanding if she got a chance to dance it. One of the company's prima ballerinas, Alexandra Danilova, also coached her in the role.

On May 1, 1943, at a matinee performance of the *Chopin Concerto* in Philadelphia, Tallchief got the chance she had waited for over so many long months. She was a great success in the role and received thunderous applause. Her letter home after the performance conveyed her joy. She wrote her family that the general director of the Ballet Russe, Jean Yazvinsky, and other leaders in the company believed that she would not always remain in the *corps de ballet*:

> *[They] think that I am the only one in the corps [de ballet] right now who looks like becoming a ballerina. Gee whiz!!! It makes me very happy. . . . I hate to have to write all this, because it makes me sound so conceited. You should have been here to see me and hear what people say for yourself.*[6]

Tallchief continued to dance the ballerina role on tour to great acclaim. After her New York debut in *Chopin Concerto*, members of the *corps de ballet* presented her with a huge bouquet of flowers. She noted in a letter home that the "kids" in the *corps* "are going around bragging about me."[7] After feeling like an outsider for so long, this was a personal as well as a professional breakthrough.

❖Maria and Marjorie❖

On a vacation home she took special pleasure in seeing her sister. Marjorie had continued studying and performing in the Los Angeles area, dancing with the ballet company headed by their former teachers, David Lichine and his wife Tatiana Riabouchinska. Tallchief hoped she could persuade her sister to join her in New York. Perhaps she thought this might help cure her own loneliness while advancing Marjorie's career. Marjorie and her mother, however, were not enthusiastic about the plans for the "kid sister" of the family to leave her position with the Lichines for the uncertainty of a place with the Ballet Russe.

Instead, Marjorie tried to convince her sister that a brighter future might lay ahead for both of them in Hollywood, where Marjorie had already landed a few small movie roles. Neither sister took the advice of the other, but the sisters remained close through letters and telephone calls even when they were thousands of miles away from each other.

The advice Tallchief received from her mother at this time was not so easily ignored, however. Mrs. Tallchief made it clear that she did not want her daughter to sign a long-term contract with the Ballet Russe. The young dancer, after all, was not in good health at the time. She was suffering from constant colds and had lost a great deal of weight since joining the company.

— ◈ —

Maria Tallchief is shown here as she appeared with the Ballet Russe in 1946 in Graduation Ball.

In some ways this was a low point for Tallchief. Yet 1944 was a turning point for her personal and professional life. It was in that year that George Balanchine joined the Ballet Russe as a choreographer. Who was this man who would dominate American dance for decades, create Tallchief's greatest roles, and eventually become her husband?

GEORGE
BALANCHINE:
CHOREOGRAPHER

George Balanchine was born on January 22,
1904, in St. Petersburg, Russia, and received the
name Georgi Melitonovich Balanchivadze.
Georgi grew up in a family where music and
religion were both "in the blood." His grandfather was a bishop in the Russian Orthodox
Church and his father was a trained singer.
Georgi's father Meliton became a member of
the opera chorus in the Russian city of Tbilisi
when he was eighteen. While performing as a

soloist with the chorus, Meliton began collecting and arranging folk songs and sacred songs from his native Georgia in Russia. This pursuit would occupy much of his later time and energy. Also around this time he got married and became the father of two children. He and his wife eventually divorced, however.

Meliton continued to study singing and composition and created the first opera ever written in the Georgian language, *Tamara the Wily*. In 1898 he married again, this time to a beautiful young woman named Maria who played the piano well. They had three children together. Georgi was the middle child of this marriage.

All of the children received piano lessons, first from their mother and then from a professional teacher. Georgi resisted the practicing that the piano demanded and would sometimes be sent to bed without supper for refusing to work at drills he found tedious. One day, while still a boy, he was working his way through a movement of one of Beethoven's sonatas and suddenly he found himself enormously moved. "[S]omething of the potential beauty and grandeur of the music suddenly came glimmering through to him. It brought tears to his eyes."[1] Just as young Betty Marie Tall Chief found the hours of drills at the bar not boring but exciting because she loved to dance so much, so too did Georgi now willingly spend as as much time as he could practicing the piano.

Andrei, Georgi's younger brother, enjoyed performing simple dances for guests at the Christmas parties and other festivities given by his parents. However, Georgi meanwhile stood "in a corner and kicked at people because he hated anything to do with dancing."[2]

Georgi's attitude was soon to change. He was nine years old when, almost by accident, he auditioned for the Imperial Theater Ballet School in St. Petersburg and was accepted. Georgi had never even seen a ballet at this time and he was often discouraged and lonely when he was unable to leave the school on weekends to be with his family.

After a short time the boy appeared with other students playing a small part in a production of Tchaikovsky's popular ballet *Sleeping Beauty*. Just as Beethoven had opened Georgi's eyes to the mystery and majesty of great music, this performance of *Sleeping Beauty* revealed to him what all his lessons at the school had been for. From this time on Georgi knew that he wanted to devote his life to dancing.[3]

Georgi began to get larger roles in school productions. When he was only sixteen, he created the choreography for *La Nuit* (The Night), a ballet set to the music of the Russian composer Anton Rubinstein. The ballet included a *pas de deux* (dance duet) including Georgi himself, and another student, Alexandra Danilova. The routine was described as "a sexy number." Danilova, who would become a well-known ballerina herself, said the dance "awakened something in me as a woman. Until then, all my boyfriends at the school had been just friends. . . . And then suddenly I thought, there is something else. . . ."[4] This passionate response to Georgi's choreography was to be reproduced in many viewers of his work in the years to come. This ballet is still performed in Russia.

Betty Marie Tall Chief would not be born for another eight years when the Russian Revolution of 1917 caused the temporary closing of the ballet school and theater where Georgi was taking classes and performing. However, both the school and the theater reopened a few years later, and Georgi was able to graduate with honors in 1921. He was asked to join the ballet company of the State Theater of Opera and Ballet. He also began intensive study of the piano and of music theory at the nearby music conservatory, and even considered a career as a composer. It was probably this study that supplied him with the background to "marry" movement and music so successfully in his choreography.

Just a year or so after graduation, Georgi began to create ballets with a dozen or so other students in what came to be called the Young Ballet Company. Among the dancers to join the group was Tamara Gevergeyeva, a blonde girl of fifteen who soon became Georgi's wife. The company's premiere performance took place in 1923 and included one work not only choreographed but also composed by Balanchine.

◈Balanchine in Europe◈

Balanchine's imaginative and unusual dances were not as popular with Russian critics and government officials as they were with the members of his company, who were devoted to him. On a trip abroad with members of the State Theater in 1924, Balanchine and his wife formally renounced their Russian citizenship and left their native country behind for good. Just as Betty Marie Tall Chief needed to leave the security of her family in Los Angeles to find a place in the world of ballet in New York City (the center of American ballet), so too did Balanchine realize that his best chance for artistic opportunity lay in Paris. Here, much of the best dancing in the world had been presented to the public since the early nineteenth century.

◈Changing His Name◈

They landed eventually in Paris with only enough money to last them a few weeks. Luckily, Sergei Diaghilev, another transplanted Russian, sought them out to join his Ballet Russe, with Georgi as dancer and choreographer. In order to make his name easier to pronounce for European audiences, Georgi Melitonovich Balanchivadze, now twenty-one years old, became George Balanchine. His title was ballet master of the Ballet Russe.

The Ballet Russe had an illustrious history. Vaslav Nijinsky is considered by some to be the century's greatest male dancer and one of its most original choreographers. During the 1910s (with several interruptions), Nijinsky toured with the troupe throughout Western Europe and North America, performing innovative ballets before enthusiastic audiences. Nijinsky lost his battle with mental illness, however, and left the company in 1921.

It was Serge Diaghilev who introduced Balanchine to another Russian defector, the composer Igor Stravinsky, and gave the young ballet master his first chance to create a ballet to Stravinsky's music. In 1925 the Ballet Russe presented *Le Chant du Rossignol* (The Song of the Nightingale) with Balanchine's choreography to an enthusiastic Paris audience, and it became a permanent part of the company's repertoire. Balanchine also created dances for over two dozen operas, including works by Stravinsky.

In 1928 Balanchine had his greatest early artistic and critical triumph with his version of the Apollo legend, set to Stravinsky's score. Balanchine himself said later: "I consider *Apollo* the turning point of my life."[5] Bernard Taper explains the unique artistic achievement Balanchine achieved with this ballet:

> *At the height of the jazz age, [Balanchine] turned to classicism—or, rather, he evolved a new*

classicism, which serenely embodied the classical virtues of clarity and grandeur and yet in spirit and in style of movement was more up to date and adventurous than the run of ultramodern ballets.[6]

One year later, in 1929, Balanchine created *Le Fils Prodigue* (The Prodigal Son), based on the Biblical story of a young man who returns after a period of wayward living to receive the blessing of his father. It was performed to the music of another famous Russian composer, Sergei Prokofiev, and was perhaps Balanchine's most moving creation to that time. Serge Lifar played the title role. According to Lifar, when the father covered his kneeling son with his cloak to signal his re-acceptance of the young man back into the family at the end of the work, "Pandemonium broke loose. . . . People were crying."[7]

❖Ballet Russe Disbands❖

Serge Diaghilev died in 1929, and the Ballet Russe was disbanded. The next few years were difficult ones for Balanchine. Apart from the collapse of his "home" company, he was on distant terms with his family in Russia and was also suffering from tuberculosis, refusing to let doctors remove the infected lung. His strength started to return after a period of recuperation, however, and he acted as guest choreographer for companies in London, Copenhagen, and Paris. He also created dances for operas put on by a new company, Ballet de Monte Carlo. In 1933 Balanchine helped to establish a Paris-based troupe known as Les Ballets.

◈Balanchine's Early Years in America◈

Balanchine always admitted to a fondness for American movies and our popular culture. He named Fred Astaire and James Cagney when he was asked which dancers he most admired.[8] In the decades to come he would choreograph many dances either based on the American experience or mixing European and American traditions. These included *Stars and Stripes,* choreographed to John Philip Sousa marches and complete with dancers representing Uncle Sam and Lady Liberty, and *Square Dance,* which featured do-si-dos and swing-your-partner steps—set to music two or three centuries old by the Italian composers Antonio Vivaldi and Arcangelo Corelli.

In 1933, the same year that Tallchief's parents moved to Los Angeles to find better musical training for their daughters, George Balanchine landed in New York City. This was a move that marked the beginning of his most important creative years. He began work as teacher and choreographer for the School of American Ballet in Manhattan on New Year's Day in 1934. His students began to offer a public program to New York audiences under the name American Ballet Company the next year. John Martin was the dance reviewer for *The New York Times* from

1927 to 1962. In the first of many critical attacks on Balanchine's early American productions, Martin found these early performances too European and promptly suggested that the choreographer, Balanchine, be dismissed.[9]

Balanchine himself was not always enthusiastic about these early productions. He later confided that in creating a ballet to Tchaikovsky's *Serenade for Strings*, for instance, he was "just trying to teach [his] students some little lessons and make a ballet which did not show how badly they danced."[10] Money was always tight in these early years. Audiences did not always appreciate that "costumes" were often little more than rehearsal clothes: male dancers some-times appeared in black tights and white t-shirts. The company also scrimped on scenery, leaving a nearly-bare stage for the dancers to perform on.

Balanchine also worked briefly creating dances for the Metropolitan Opera (the "Met") in Manhattan. Balanchine produced dances for no fewer than thirteen operas during the Met's 1935–1936 season. However, the forward-looking choreography Balanchine favored did not go over well with the more conservative management and audience of America's outstanding opera company.

The ballet master of the American Ballet and the "Met" parted company after just a few years. Before that happened, though, Balanchine presented a major festival of ballets set to Stravinsky's music for the stage of the Metropolitan Opera in 1937.

For a time it seemed that Balanchine's future might actually be as a choreographer for Broadway shows. In 1936 two hit musical comedies premiered on Broadway with dances partly by Balanchine: the *Ziegfeld Follies* and *On Your Toes*. *On Your Toes* included one of Richard Rodgers's most famous compositions, "Slaughter on Tenth Avenue," a violent tale told entirely in dance that stopped the show every night.

Balanchine followed this Broadway triumph with dances for another show the next year, Richard Rodgers's *Babes in Arms*. This production included the first "dream ballet" ever seen in an American musical. With choreography for three Broadway hits behind him, who could say now that Balanchine did not know how to produce "American" dances? In the next few years, several more Broadway shows (including *Cabin in the Sky*) featured Balanchine dances.

◈To California◈

In 1937 Betty Marie Tall Chief was twelve years old and studying with Bronislava Nijinska in Beverly Hills, California. That same year Balanchine traveled to California to create several dances for the musical movie extravaganza *The Goldwyn Follies*. The most impressive dancing in the movie was set to George

— ❖ —

George Balanchine, who was married to Maria Tallchief from 1946 to 1951, was perhaps the most acclaimed and influential choreographer in America. He created many of Tallchief's most memorable dances.

Gershwin's *An American in Paris* and starred Vera Zorina, whom Balanchine married in 1938. The couple also worked together on dances for the Hollywood version of *On Your Toes*, which appeared the next year. Balanchine became an American citizen in this year as well.

In the early 1940s Balanchine accepted choreography assignments from the touring ballet company Lincoln Kirstein had formed, the American Ballet Caravan. He created two new ballets for the company's four-month-long South American tour. In 1942 he served as guest director of ballet at the Teatro Colón in Buenos Aires, Argentina. In 1944 George Balanchine joined the Ballet Russe de Monte Carlo as choreographer.

◈Balanchine's Place in Modern Dance◈

Balanchine created approximately one hundred fifty ballets in America using many different styles over his long career. Some had exciting dramatic stories from ancient sources (such as *The Firebird* and *The Prodigal Son*), others were filled with glamour and romance (for instance, *Night Shadow,* with music from Bellini's opera *La Sonnambula*). Balanchine's most typical choreography, however, used so-called "pure dance." As Walter Terry explains in his *Ballet Companion*, these are works (such as *Theme and Variations* set to music by Peter Tchaikovsky) "with no story, no plot, no characters other than the dancers themselves. . . . These are ballets best described as dance for the sake of dancing."[11]

The "pure dance" that Balanchine made such an important element of his works sometimes lacked obvious stories or complex fictional characters to keep the attention of the audience. This did not however make them dry or lacking in fire and excitement. The famous dance critic Edwin Denby wrote that the emotions Balanchine reveals in his choreography "are like those of Mozart, tender, joyous and true. He leaves the audience with a civilized happiness. His art is peaceful and exciting, as classical art has always been."[12]

Maria Tallchief had chosen to concentrate on dance after an exceptionally promising beginning as a concert pianist provided her with an extensive musical background. George Balanchine, like Tallchief, had a rare sensitivity to the music he used in his dance routines. He made it an equal partner in his works. For instance, he often collaborated closely with composers of new scores. He created no fewer than thirty-nine dances to music of Igor Stravinsky. Stravinsky asserted, "To see Balanchine's ballets is to hear the music with one's eyes."[13]

Balanchine even believed that his choreography could lead the audience back to a new appreciation of the music he used. He wrote of his classic ballet *Symphonie Concertante* (which was in the "pure dance" style and in which Maria Tallchief was a principal dancer at the premiere in 1947):

> *This ballet is a good example of how dancing might aid appreciation of the music. Mozart's [music] is long and difficult; to the inexperienced listener it might be boring. . . . The ballet, on the other hand, fills the time measured by music with movement and seems to shorten the length of the music. What seemed dull at a first hearing, is not so dull when the ballet is first seen.*[14]

Ballet is a combination of sound, movement, and drama. George Balanchine had the rare gift of being able to construct dances that mixed magnificent music and expressive, innovative dance movements with a theatrical flair that thrilled audiences for decades. Balanchine "was a poet," Tallchief has said, "and he taught us how to react and become this poetry."[15]

Balanchine dominated American dance until his death in 1983, and his choreography is still performed around the world. It was with Maria Tallchief that he was first able to reach a large audience with a dancer raised and trained in the United States.

Tallchief and Balanchine

The first time Maria Tallchief worked with George Balanchine was during the summer of 1944. He choreographed dances for the Broadway musical *Song of Norway*, based on the life of Edvard Grieg. "I was invited to go on Broadway with the show, but decided not to because I wanted desperately to be a ballet dancer," Tallchief recalled almost forty years later.[1]

Marjorie, meanwhile, had joined the Lichines at the Ballet Theatre in New York City.

Tallchief had always felt like a protector to her "baby sister," but she recalled that she had been "dumbfounded to find Marjorie grown up," with a mind of her own.[2] As Tallchief's biographer Olga Maynard wrote:

> Marjorie refused to take life, even ballet too seriously; Maria, née Betty Marie, made everything, especially dancing, a life-and-death matter. Sadly she renounced her loving role of dominant older sister, but she would never quite lose the motherly anxiety and affection for the baby, Marjorie.[3]

❖Comparing Sisters❖

The sisters continued to resemble each other even as they grew into full adulthood, but critics saw important differences in their styles. Marjorie was praised especially for her high spirits and rapid, precise movements, all in a clear, classical presentation. Maria, on the other hand, was seen by some critics as more "the strong, chilly technician" with a larger "symphonic" style. However, other viewers were struck by the elder Tallchief's "passion and fire." She would grow into "a classicist of strong technique, with a romantic beauty."[4]

Marjorie worked for several companies during the next twenty years. When she felt she was no longer progressing as she wished, she had no hesitation in looking for a company where she could advance her artistry and continue to learn.[5] In 1947 Marjorie found an ideal partner both professionally and personally after joining the Grand Ballet du Marquis de Cuevas. She married George Skibine in 1947 in Vichy, France. Both her sister and Balanchine attended the ceremony.

Marjorie was usually paired with her husband during their nine years with the Paris-based Cuevas company and often later as well. The couple had twin sons, Alex and George. Aunt Maria doted on her nephews and even learned French so she could speak to the boys, who were raised in France.

Marjorie became a member of the Théâtre National Opéra in Paris in the late 1950s, where she was *première danseuse* (first female dancer) while Skibine was the star male dancer in the company as well as choreographer. In the 1960s Marjorie performed with the Ruth Page Chicago Opera Ballet, the Russian Bolshoi, and New York Harkness Ballet. She taught dance for several years after her retirement in 1966.

Between 1944 and 1946 Balanchine created six productions for the Ballet Russe. The first was called *Danses Concertantes*. It was the first ballet in which Maria Tallchief danced to the music of Igor Stravinsky. Balanchine choreographed two starring, so-called *premières,* or "first" roles for Tallchief in 1946. These would give her the chance to create characters and show off her talents to full effect. The couple also started to see each other socially, outside of the classroom and rehearsal hall, at this time.

Tallchief played the title character in *Le Baiser de la Fée* (The Kiss of the Fairy). It was loosely based on Hans Christian Andersen's story "The Ice Queen." Tallchief called it "one of the most fascinating roles I ever danced" with its high "drama and beautiful *pas de deux* [duet]."[6] She also created the starring *coquette* (flirt) role in *Night Shadow*, performed to music by the nineteenth-century Italian opera composer Vincenzo Bellini.

By 1943 Tallchief began to take all of her lessons outside of the Ballet Russe from the School of American Ballet, founded by Balanchine and Lincoln Kirstein in 1934. Tallchief believed that Balanchine was able to combine traditional (classical) ballet movements with the freer style of popular American dance and to encourage his dancers to push themselves past what they thought were their natural limits. Balanchine's idea of "classical dance" combined control *and* passion, the best of European and American movements. As Tallchief put it:

> *In my mind [Balanchine] has taken his own classical training . . . and combined it with the American, rangy [filled with loose movement] way of moving. . . . To me it's just good classical dancing. It's a way of timing, of attacking, of not holding back, of giving every ounce of your energy. You're never comfortable. To be comfortable and careful—that's not dancing.*[7]

❖Tallchief and Balanchine Marry❖

Only one month after Balanchine's resignation from the Ballet Russe, on August 16, 1946, he and Maria Tallchief married. Tallchief's parents were as shocked as the members of the company. None had suspected how close the choreographer and dancer had become. Her parents had moved back to Fairfax, Oklahoma, after Tallchief's father had become ill. Now their "little girl" was becoming the wife of a man who had been married three times before and was more than twice her age.

The years between the marriage and Tallchief's acceptance into Balanchine's New York City Ballet (originally Ballet Society) were difficult ones. Her contract with the Ballet Russe committed her to that company until 1947. Tallchief hurt her foot during her last seasons with the Ballet Russe and was unable to dance at many performances. She would join her husband briefly in 1947 when Balanchine presented some of his ballets with the Paris Opera. Yet Tallchief and her husband were working for rival ballet companies when they desperately wanted to work together.

The Ballet Society was a struggling company when Maria Tallchief joined it in 1947. On April 28 of that year, though, Balanchine presented the premiere of *Orpheus.* This was a ballet, with music by Igor Stravinsky, starring Maria Tallchief. The work created an immediate sensation. Stravinsky, the leading composer

— ❖ —

Maria Tallchief is shown in her rehearsal robe with George Balanchine, her mentor and husband (1946–1951), on the left.

of the twentieth century, conducted the orchestra at the first performance. The story tells of how the heroic Orpheus follows his beloved Eurydice into the underworld. Unable to resist looking back at her as he leads her back to life, he sacrifices both their lives.

Tallchief's "proud and mysterious" Eurydice, as one critic described it, won the dancer the Annual *Dance Magazine* Award.[8] In presenting her with this honor, the American dance world's most influential magazine praised Tallchief for her "memorable lyric quality, for a discipline beautiful to see, for command and growing compassion."[9]

◈The New York City Ballet◈

Building on this success, The Ballet Society found a permanent home at New York's City Center. It also changed its named to The New York City Ballet. Even with the triumph of *Orpheus,* however, the company had difficulty during the first year. It could not find a large enough audience to support its efforts. Tallchief also took time off to dance with the rival Ballet Theatre.

Stravinsky, Balanchine, and Maria Tallchief again collaborated during the fall season of 1949 on the ballet *The Firebird.* The premiere of *The Firebird* took place on November 27, 1949. Tallchief's performance shot her to fame within the dance world, and the ballet provided the company with its greatest popular success up to that time (see Chapter 1). Critics singled out Tallchief for special praise.

Doris Hering, for instance, wrote in *Dance Magazine* that Tallchief's dancing was "maddeningly beautiful and somehow not quite human" and that she showed "an almost frightening technical range."[10] An article in *Newsweek* stated that Tallchief's "dazzling" *Firebird* was "so sure, strong, and brilliant that it is doubtful if her superior as a technician exists anywhere today."[11]

At last The New York City Ballet, under the artistic direction of Tallchief's husband George Balanchine, was at the very center of a ballet revival. Balanchine had created a company with Tallchief, a homegrown star, at its center. Now the company was drawing large audiences, delighting the critics, and making Maria Tallchief internationally famous—even among people who had never seen a ballet. Despite many triumphs as a dancer, though, Tallchief would face several personal disappointments in the years ahead.

Tallchief's growth as an artist and as a "dance actor" during the next decade have assured her a permanent place among the great ballerinas of the century. Many people who saw her perform live or on television even forty or fifty years ago maintain a fresh impression of her power and passion as a dancer.

Pigeon Crowle, in *Enter the Ballerina*, has given an estimation of how much Tallchief had achieved and (even after her spirited, even inspired, performance

— ◈ —

Maria Tallchief is shown here in her most famous role as the title character in George Balanchine's production of The Firebird, *which premiered in 1949.*

in *The Firebird*) how far she still had to go in the late 1940s:

> *As yet she lacked depth and warmth of feeling, and expressed her emotions almost entirely in movement, while her interesting face was closed against warmth and play of expression. Even so, her easy balance and her incredibly fluid technique . . . seemed to have no limit. . . .*[12]

❖Critics Speak❖

By the 1950s, some critics started to remark on Tallchief's versatility as a dancer as well as on her achievements in individual works. Writing in 1956, Walter Terry praised her "endless visions of impossible difficult actions accomplished with consummate ease . . . [combining] the bearing of a princess with the physical prowess of an athlete." Then, within a single paragraph, Terry described Tallchief's dancing in Balanchine productions as "a stream of fire [which] circles the stage" in the *Firebird;* marveled at her "incredible swiftness" dancing in *Symphony in C;* talked of her body "slash[ing]" the air in *Four Temperaments;* admired her "delicacy and tenderness" in *Scotch Symphony;* and detailed her part in the "tortured and exquisitely sad" dance version of the Orpheus legend.[13]

Edwin Denby was another dance critic who watched Tallchief's artistic development during the 1940s and 1950s. He reviewed Tallchief's performance in *Ballet Imperial* with the Ballet Russe de Monte

Carlo in 1945 by pointing out that she was a "real star," "brilliant in speed and with a steely exactness."[14] Eight years later Denby was critical of her dancing to music with slow tempos. But among those dancing classical ballet in passages that required speed, Tallchief was the boldest and "the most correctly brilliant," able to "lift a ballet by an entrance."[15]

In 1965 Tallchief was herself asked what quality was most essential to a ballerina. She might have named any of the qualities that had matured in her over the years: a sense of style, dedication to improvement, ability to learn and grow, sensitivity to the music, even the refusal to give up in the face of obstacles. Rather, she answered:

> *Mystery is an important quality. The viewer should not be able to anticipate what is coming next, for then the excitement, the revealing are gone. So what we have to guard against in ballet is peopling the stage with a bunch of machines.*[16]

Maria Tallchief has never been accused of dancing mechanically, although critics sometimes found her technical mastery overshadowing the emotional appeal dance can provide. As she matured as a woman, her dancing began to portray new depths of passion, and ultimately, the mystery that makes a dancer unique.

TALLCHIEF AS PRIMA BALLERINA

Forty-six dancers from The New York City Ballet traveled to London in the summer of 1950. The tour was a disappointment for the company and for Maria Tallchief. The stage at London's Covent Garden was huge compared to the one in New York. The surface of the floor was so rough that the dancers' toe shoes were constantly tearing. The ballets that made such an overwhelming impression on a small stage were lost in the "cavern" of Covent Garden.

Even *The Firebird* received only polite applause. Tallchief hoped that Balanchine's *Serenade,* in which she also had a starring role, would find a more enthusiastic reception. She tore a ligament, however, near the start of the ballet and had to be replaced by another dancer.

The six-week tour of England struggled on without its biggest star. Her ankle would not heal and she was also suffering from a serious intestinal sickness. In all, the company lost forty thousand dollars on the English engagements. The mood of the dancers is reflected in a letter that one of them wrote home at this time: "We do better to stay at City Center, where people understand Balanchine's ballets, than to wander in the cold, crool [sic] world."[1]

The marriage between George Balanchine and Maria Tallchief only lasted from 1946 to 1951, ending in an annulment. Still Tallchief continued to dance in new ballets created for her by Balanchine until 1960. This was to be the decade of her greatest fame and professional success.

Tallchief and Balanchine shared many good times together in their five years of marriage. They would often play duets on matching grand pianos in their apartment. Balanchine could talk about preparing food at great length, "almost to the point of boredom."[2] The couple also divided up many unglamorous tasks around the house. Tallchief remembers the years of their marriage mostly as a time of no-nonsense hard work and simple living. Almost forty years after her wedding, Tallchief recalled:

> *George and I lived in a five-floor walk-up. There was no luxury in our lives. We didn't need any because we spent the whole time in the studio— got there at nine in the morning and left at ten at night. We had a sandwich at Sammy's Delicatessen, and that was our life.*[3]

Some tensions were revealed early in the marriage. Balanchine grew irritated on being ordered to walk on newspapers after Tallchief had scrubbed the floor, or when she invited other dancers over for a game of poker, which Balanchine did not play. People who knew them remarked that they were seldom alone together. Both often preferred to spend time with their own friends.[4]

❖Marriage in Trouble❖

It was while on tour in England that Tallchief realized that her marriage with Balanchine was in serious trouble. She promptly moved out of the London apartment. As one biographer of Balanchine puts it, "Maria had a very strong character and was not prepared to stand for any nonsense."[5] She was respected for this quality and her dancing.

When the company returned to New York, Balanchine helped Tallchief find another apartment with another dancer, Vida Brown. In 1951 the marriage was legally annulled. The grounds for the annulment were officially that Balanchine refused to allow Tallchief to have a child. Almost thirty years later, Tallchief explained the failure of their marriage this way: "I realize now I was just too young to be married to a genius."[6] Tallchief did not ask for alimony from Balanchine. Newspapers reported that she would support herself as a dancer. Tallchief remembers that she would sometimes travel directly from the courthouse where her divorce was being considered to her dance rehearsals with Balanchine. "George was choreographing *Scotch Symphony* on me and we *had* to rehearse! So what was important was the work. Nothing else mattered."[7] Despite the fact that they were no longer married, Tallchief continued dancing for Balanchine into the 1960s.

❖Short Second Marriage❖

Maria Tallchief met her second husband in 1951. He was a dashing charter airplane pilot named Elmourza Natirboff. Natirboff was not interested in ballet. He finally demanded that Tallchief choose between the marriage and her career. She made the difficult choice and the marriage ended in a divorce in 1954 after just two years.

In 1951, Tallchief danced the role of the Queen of the Swans in Balanchine's production of *Swan Lake*, which is set to one of Peter Tchaikovsky's most beautiful scores. *Swan Lake* is, with *The Nutcracker* (another dance to Tchaikovsky's music), one of the most popular classical ballets. Tallchief herself remembers her disappointment with her first performance of the role and the encouragement she received from Felia Doubrovska, a retired ballet dancer:

> *I remember I danced badly my first* Swan Lake. *It was a nerve-wracking experience, and it didn't go well that night. At one o'clock in the morning after the first performance my phone rang and it was Felia Doubrovska. She said, "I just want you to know, Maria, maybe you're not too happy tonight. But it was nerves." And it was true.*[8]

Tallchief danced "The Dying Swan" solo from *Swan Lake* in the 1952 Metro-Goldwyn-Mayer film biography of swimmer Annette Kellerman, *Million Dollar Mermaid*. She appeared as the legendary ballerina Anna Pavlova. When she rehearsed the sequence for the film's director as Balanchine had created it, the director was less than enthusiastic. "Sorry, Miss Tallchief, this won't do," he told her, "The number is too quiet, not spectacular enough. Please do some fast turns and jumps so that the audience will have something to look at."[9] Dying swans and "fast turns and jumps" might not appear to go very well together, but Tallchief managed to please the film's director and still maintain much of the beauty and deep feeling of the role.

❖Television Premier❖

Television was fairly new in the early 1950s. Maria Tallchief made her television debut in 1952. She appeared on "The Blue Ribbon Christmas Eve

Musical." By the end of the decade, Tallchief would appear on television many times. She performed solos and duets on such programs as *Hallmark Hall of Fame, Omnibus,* and *The Ed Sullivan Show.*

During a European tour in 1952, Tallchief proved that it had just been "nerves" that kept her from doing her best as the Swan Queen. Beginning in Zurich, Switzerland, and continuing to several other cities, Tallchief's performance with her partner André Eglevsky was pronounced "the performance of a lifetime" by one European critic. Tallchief received fifteen curtain calls from an enthusiastic audience at one performance.[10] Another European admirer wrote that Tallchief "thrills the spirit, moves the heart, and brings to the eyes the tears that cannot be withheld, not only for the Swan Queen, but from the knowledge that this is a lovely and perfect thing."[11] After the disastrous London tour of two years before and her personal disappointment at the New York premiere of *Swan Lake,* her triumphant European tour was a sweet success.

◆Tallchief Honored◆

By the time the company returned to America in September 1952, Tallchief was perhaps the most famous Oklahoman. The State Legislature declared June 29, 1953, "Maria Tallchief Day." Oklahoma's governor made her a staff colonel and even pronounced her a "commodore" of the Oklahoma Navy. (Both were honorary titles; Oklahoma does not really have a navy.)

Tallchief's parents had returned to Fairfax, Oklahoma, by this time and the Osage were especially proud of their "favorite daughter." The Osage Tribal Council held a morning reception for Tallchief and her family. Traditional dishes like "fry bread," beef cooked with dried corn, and steamed beef were served and Osage dances were performed in her honor. Tallchief's grandmother Eliza had told her and her sister about Osage history, traditional stories and ceremonial dances when they were children. Now Eliza chose a special name for her granddaughter: *Wa-Xthe-Thonba*, meaning "Woman of Two Standards." This symbolized Tallchief's mixed heritage. Dressed in an ornate Osage outfit and crowned with a headdress of feathers and beadwork, Tallchief became an honorary leader of the Osage people, a position especially created for her.

Tallchief was proud to be so honored for her heritage, but she was also committed to the world of ballet. As she later explained with a touch of humor, "I really do feel more comfortable in a ballet crown than in feathers!"[12]

❖ *The Nutcracker* ❖

The newly-named Osage "princess" returned to the New York City Ballet in 1954. She scored a triumph in Balanchine's new production of *The Nutcracker* as the Sugar Plum Fairy, one of classical ballet's most challenging roles. Tallchief's biographer, Olga Maynard, believes that the dancer achieved a new level of "authority and radiance" in the role of the Sugar Plum Fairy. She displayed "an almost quivering, ever-perceptive intelligence." This combined with her physical beauty and technical brilliance to make her an even greater artist. Her emotional impact also deepened in the role, Maynard believes: "the beautiful woman, the gracious dancer had a softer manner which in no way detracted from glittering attributes."[13]

The New York City Ballet was one of the first companies to list the dancers alphabetically, not putting the stars first. Audiences did not even know which dancers would be performing on any given night. This was done to encourage them "to attend programs that were interesting and not to follow individual dancers."[14] Tallchief once commented that she didn't mind being *listed* alphabetically as long as she wasn't *treated* alphabetically.[15] Audiences who were lucky enough to attend one of her performances certainly did not respond to her "alphabetically." She and Balanchine's inspired choreography were for many dance lovers the main reasons they continued to support the New York City Ballet.

Tallchief took a leave of absence from the New York City Ballet in 1954 to tour with the Ballet Russe. It had been five years since her last American tour with the Ballet Theatre. She was offered the highest

— ❖ —

Maria Tallchief wears her costume as the Sugar Plum Fairy in Balanchine's production of The Nutcracker, *with music by Peter Tchaikovsky. It had its first performance in 1954.*

weekly salary ever offered to a ballerina up to that time—two thousand dollars. The sold-out, enthusiastic audiences in over one hundred cities proved that the money was well spent.

Despite her acclaim and the flattering amount of her salary, Tallchief later told an interviewer she never should have taken the leave of absence. "I shouldn't have done it. It was a mistake, and I was very unhappy," she confessed. "Practically all I danced was *Scheherazade.* And then I hurt my foot. I rejoined the New York City Ballet right away."[16]

After returning to the New York City Ballet, she joined international tours. By 1960 they had taken her to Europe (five times), Japan, South America, the Middle East, and the Soviet Union. In fact, Tallchief attained an even greater artistic status abroad than she did at home.

Even so, American critics were sometimes at a loss for words in assessing her achievement. John Martin of *The New York Times*, who had criticized elements of Tallchief's dancing before, now despaired trying to find words to match her artistry. "It is useless to remark on an artist's qualities," Martin wrote in one review, "when the artist has reached the degree of maturity that Tallchief has."[17]

❖Third Marriage❖

Tallchief became a bride for the third and final time in 1956. She had met Henry D. "Buzzy" Paschen, Jr., two years earlier when she ". . . was invited to the yacht club, and here was this handsome sailor."[18]

Henry Paschen was two years younger than Tallchief. In 1956 he was a purchasing officer in his family's construction business. Paschen had served for two years in the United States Army after World War II. He had gotten a degree from DePaul University in Chicago. An avid sportsman (tennis, golf, and skiing), Paschen also had an intense interest in opera and ballet. He was so moved by Tallchief's dying swan in *Swan Lake* that he cried backstage during one performance.

By 1956, the New York City Ballet had changed and, with her marriage to Henry Paschen, Maria Tallchief had changed as well. Balanchine's wife of four years, the ballerina Tanaquil Le Clercq, contracted polio and Balanchine left the company to spend more time with her. Henry Paschen appreciated his new wife's talent and clearly loved the world of dance, but he hoped that his new wife would give up her career as a dancer and become a full-time wife, and eventually a mother. So, Tallchief had both professional and personal reasons when she made her decision to leave the New York City Ballet, at least temporarily, to join her husband in Chicago in 1956. Now she could try to add the satisfactions of her marriage to her list of achievements as America's prima ballerina.

THE END OF A GREAT CAREER

Tallchief continued to appear at engagements around the United States in the mid- and late-1950s. In the summer of 1957, she danced a *pas de deux* from *Scotch Symphony* with her New York City Ballet partner André Eglevsky. It was on a program at the Jacob's Pillow Dance Festival in Massachusetts. On the same program, Tom Two Arrows (Thomas J. Dorsey), an Iroquois dancer dressed in leather moccasins, trousers of buckskin, and porcupine quills fashioned into an elaborate headdress, performed traditional dances. They danced in separate parts of the program. Taken together, Tallchief and Tom Two Arrows displayed how two dancers with Native American heritage could excel in performing two very different kinds of dancing. Tallchief's mastery of classical ballet based on European traditions as adapted by George Balanchine contrasted with Two Arrows's rhythmic harvest and fertility dances, with names such as "Husk Face Dance" and "Eagle Dance."

In October 1957, Tallchief appeared with three other famous Native American dancers from Oklahoma (Rosella Hightower, Yvonne Chouteau, and Moscelyne Larkin) at the Oklahoma Indian Ballerina Festival in Tulsa, Oklahoma. They were there to commemorate the fiftieth anniversary of Oklahoma's statehood. Tallchief's sister Marjorie and her husband George Skibine were unable to attend. They were committed to a command dance perfor-mance for the President of France during the two days of Oklahoma festivities.

Tallchief was again paired with her New York City Ballet partner André Eglevsky to open the program with the second act of *Swan Lake*. Also attending as spectators were Tallchief's brother and her parents, who traveled from Fairfax to see their daughter per-form. It was, of course, Tallchief's mother who had sought out the best musical training for both of her daughters when they were girls. She had a simple answer, however, when a reporter at the festival asked her "What makes a ballerina?" "They're born, not made," she replied.[1] Mrs. Tallchief also confided that she would "rather play bridge than eat" and that her husband, who had earlier held an official position involving Osage affairs, now enjoyed playing golf as often as possible.[2]

❖Motherhood❖

Maria Tallchief gave birth to her only child, Elise Maria, on January 4, 1959. Tallchief resigned temporarily from the New York City Ballet in 1960. She continued to dance even as a new mother, however. She appeared again at Jacob's Pillow in Massachusetts and on tour with the American Ballet Theater in Europe and the Soviet Union. Partnered with the Danish dancer Erik Bruhn, she received some of the best reviews of her career at the Annual Gala of the British Royal Academy of Dance in December of 1960. One critic wrote of her *pas de deux* with Bruhn from *Swan Lake*:

> [B]ecause of the essence of the individual artists and the rare beauty of the physical partnership, nothing today surpasses, or even rivals, the passion and grace of Tallchief and Bruhn.[3]

In April 1961 Tallchief attempted a completely new kind of role, one that proved how much she had grown as a dramatic actress as well as a dancer. Some critics had always believed that Tallchief's dancing had a "chilly" quality, that she downplayed the dramatic elements in a dance and highlighted the dazzling precision and self-control she had worked so hard to master. *Miss Julie*, based on a bleak drama by the Swedish playwright August Strindberg, was a complete departure from the classical and modern ballet roles on which she had made her reputation. The title character portrayed by Tallchief in *Miss Julie* was a cruel and unhappy woman in a well-to-do family. She dominates her fiancé and humiliates (and seduces) the family butler before finally killing herself in despair. Tallchief dominated the stage and moved many members of the audience to tears as the doomed heroine of the ballet. Walter Terry asked in his review of the dance for the *New York Herald Tribune*, "What can one say when faced with the closest to perfection that dancing mortals can achieve?"[4]

Dance Magazine presented Tallchief with one of its annual awards in 1961. A critic on the magazine's staff, Doris Hering, emphasized the range of Tallchief's achievement, from the classical perfection demanded by Balanchine to "a kind of sharpness, a bite, an attack, and a fierceness that was quite amazing" in her performance in *Miss Julie*.[5]

❖Tallchief Retires❖

Tallchief continued to perform with the New York City Ballet and other companies in the early 1960s. By

— ❖ —

Maria Tallchief is shown here as she appeared on tour with the American Ballet Theatre in 1961.

1965, however, younger dancers were dominating the spotlight. Balanchine was now creating his new dances for others to introduce. Not since 1960 had Tallchief danced the premiere of a Balanchine work. She left the company in 1965 and formally retired from dancing in 1966.

Walter Terry explained the New York City Ballet's unusual policy toward the dancers of the company around 1965, when Tallchief resigned. In an art form where the public often attends a performance to see a certifiable "star," "George Balanchine [and the New York City Ballet] is disinterested in stars (casts are never announced in advance) and places the accent upon the junior performers."[6]

Making a distinction between a *ballet dancer* and a true *ballerina*, Tallchief asserted that the New York City Ballet neither needed nor wanted a ballerina in 1965 and noted that she was often only to be seen at "early bird" matinees.[7] Her bitterness can be felt as she continued:

> *I resent the definition that a ballerina is an 'old bag,' for ours is a life of dedication. . . . Of course, we need new dancers, new bodies, new souls on the stage, but we need the youngsters to master the classics.*
>
> *We also need these youngsters, these newcomers to respect and learn from those who have achieved stature in their art. . . .*
>
> *What finally happened was that I was not given the kind of support I needed as a performer—I was not given a chance to serve. Also*

— ◈ —

Maria Tallchief's dancing gained in dramatic power over the years, as this close-up from the 1960s shows.

*my dignity was imperiled—this, perhaps, was the
all-important factor in my decision.*[8]

Some critics believe that Maria Tallchief was right
to leave the world of dance performers and concentrate on teaching when she did. Author Robert Garis
has written that after returning to the New York City
Ballet in 1962, Tallchief's "distinctive power was
gone." She gradually improved, according to Garis,
and deserved the status of senior ballerina in the
company until 1965. She was no longer, however, "a
dancer who created major experiences."[9]

Tallchief's interest in the arts continued. She
served on the Woman's Board of the Chicago Civic
Opera Company and gave dance instruction to members of the company. She also became director for a
time of the Indian Council Fire Achievement Award,
Inc., which presents an annual award to notable
Native Americans. She supported the local Indian
Center in Illinois. Popular on the college lecture
circuit, she also gave seminars on dance and partici-
pated in conferences in Native American cultural
studies.

Looking back in 1966 at her "fantastic" dance
career, Tallchief declared:

*It was marvelous doing what I loved to do well
enough so that I gave people pleasure. But it was
lonely, being a ballerina—and terribly demanding,
as I knew from the beginning it would be.*[10]

The next three decades would give Tallchief the opportunity to trade the "terribly demanding" role of *prima ballerina* for the roles of wife and mother, ballet teacher to young people, and with her husband, supporter both artistically and financially of the arts in Chicago.

A Busy Retirement

By the early 1970s Tallchief's daughter, Elise Marie, had begun studying ballet. According to her mother, however, she showed more promise and interest in the piano. This was just the reverse of Tallchief, whose early love of ballet had to take second place to her training as a concert pianist until she was in her teens.

◈Teaching in Chicago◈

Beginning in 1973 Tallchief became director of Chicago's Lyric Opera Ballet and its school. She began in 1972 by teaching members of the Lyric Opera to enter and exit the stage with grace and poise. As director, she spent up to eight hours a day training over a dozen young members of the troupe. They had to learn to perform the ballet sequences that the operas demanded. Even in the late 1970s, when Tallchief was in her mid-fifties, she continued to do an hour of dance exercises every morning. She also taught her students the lessons of dedication to the craft that had made her a star. "Training is everything—it's all work and muscle memory," she told a reporter around this time.[1]

The Chicago Lyric Opera began to feature more and more ambitious dancing, including choreography created by George Balanchine for the operas *Faust* and *Orpheus and Eurydice*. One local reviewer gave an encouraging evaluation of Tallchief's influence in 1979, writing:

> *Tallchief has done her job well. Her dancers give eagerly of what they have learned in the studio and classroom, and their confidence now seems to be growing out of a clear vision of where they are headed, not just of where they have been.*[2]

In December 1979, however, the Chicago Lyric Opera was having financial problems. Budget cuts led to the end of ballet instruction at the company. Tallchief was asked to return her key to the dance studio where she had worked so hard training her students. Three years later, she remembered her sense of sadness and sense of loyalty to the young people in her classes:

> We were in the depths of despair. . . . We had no place to go. I felt so awful for the dancers who had stayed here with me through thick and thin. They were very loyal. I could not betray the confidence they had in me.[3]

In 1980 Henry Paschen, now president of Paschen Construction, Inc., came to the rescue. He offered studio space in a building he owned for what became the Chicago City Ballet and School. Beginning with lecture-demonstrations in Chicago's Urban Gateways program, the young company started performing wherever they could: a suburban hall in Evanston, Illinois, the outdoor shell in Chicago's Grant Park, at downtown Daley Plaza. Soon, the Lyric Opera saw what they had lost by not having trained dancers to perform in their productions. Members of the Chicago City Ballet began to appear in many Lyric operas.

Maria Tallchief became artistic director of the Chicago City Ballet. She chose as her assistant Paul Mejia, a Peruvian-born dancer and choreographer who had begun creating dances at the age of fourteen. Tallchief's sister Marjorie, who had enjoyed a long dance career of her own until 1966, lost her husband (and frequent partner) George Skibine in 1981. She then joined Tallchief as a teacher at the Chicago City Ballet.

By this time there were twenty-six dancers under contract for a forty-four week season. Joseph Krakora, general director of the group, managed to raise almost $1,500,000 from public sources and individuals interested in bringing a full-time ballet company to Chicago.

The Chicago City Ballet toured the Midwest during much of the 1980s, and gave summer performances at the Newport Music Festival. Audiences, critics, and even politicians seemed delighted. Then-mayor of Chicago Jane Byrne said, "Chicago supports a world-renowned symphony orchestra and a highly acclaimed opera company. . . . [and] The Chicago City Ballet has the character and the talent" to make Chicago a center for ballet, too.[4]

Paul Mejia co-artistic director (with Tallchief) of the Chicago City Ballet since 1981, left the company in the spring of 1987. The search committee looking for a replacement for Mejia chose Daniel Duell, a principal dancer with the New York City Ballet. Tallchief did not attend the rehearsals for the works Duell was preparing for the fall season or the performances themselves. The company's administrators then decided to change Tallchief's title from "co-artistic director" to "artistic advisor" without her knowledge or approval.

Tallchief's husband, who owned the building housing the company's studios and offices, evicted the ten administrators and twenty-six dancers of the company. Members of the company found out in November of 1987 that paychecks would no longer be guaranteed after the middle of that month. The dancers tried to put off the inevitable by planning benefits for the thirteen-year-old company. Without the financial support of Maria Tallchief and her husband, however, Chicago lost its only commercial ballet company.

After the disappointing outcome of Tallchief's efforts to maintain the Chicago City Ballet, Tallchief re-established her relationship with the Lyric Opera Ballet School of Chicago. She has continued participating in activities at the Chicago school into the 1990s.

Tallchief continued teaching in the late 1980s after the end of the Chicago City Ballet at her own School for the Chicago Ballet. In 1989, Hugh Boulware of the *Chicago Tribune* reported that "At [sixty-five], Maria Tallchief still has the lean legs of a prima ballerina and the dramatic presence one would expect from a great actress."[5] She continued to teach Balanchine's methods to her students. Tallchief told Boulware a story that gives a hint of the pleasure—and price—of her energetic life. ". . . [Y]ou're going to get arthritis when you've been so physically active. As my [pharmacist] said the other day, 'You're now paying for all those years.' But he said, 'It was worth it, wasn't it?' and I said, 'It certainly was.'"[6]

❖Beautiful Homes❖

Maria Tallchief's home life proved to be a great source of happiness to her. Three of the homes owned by her and her husband were featured in *Architectural Digest* in the 1980s: the twenty-fourth-floor residence on Chicago's "Gold Coast" (Lake Shore Drive) with its seventeenth-century Aubusson tapestry and modern works by Rene Magritte and Max Ernst; the summer house on Martha's Vineyard in Massachusetts, with a circular deck overlooking the Vineyard Sound where the couple stand outside at the end of the day "watching the sunset and the moon come out on the other side of the sky;" and a brownstone near New York City's Lincoln Center.[7] Elise Marie would often entertain her own friends at her parents' homes in the 1980s. She was back from attending Harvard University as an undergraduate and studying modern poetry at Oxford University as a graduate student.

❖Mural Unveiled❖

In November 1991 Tallchief was honored by the state of Oklahoma. Native American artist Mike Larsen unveiled his mural *Flight of the Spirit* in its permanent home at the state capitol building. In this huge painting (a semicircle with maximum dimensions of twenty-two by twelve feet), Larsen, himself a member of the Chickasaw tribe, portrayed five Native

— ❖ —

The "Five Indian Ballerinas of Oklahoma" are honored with the permanent installation of Mike Larsen's mural Flight of the Spirit *at the Oklahoma state capitol building in 1991. In the second row, from left to right are: Yvonne Chouteau, Rosella Hightower, Maria Tallchief, Marjorie Tallchief, and Moscelyne Larkin.*

American ballerinas born in Oklahoma. All five (Maria and Marjorie Tallchief, Yvonne Chouteau, Rosella Hightower, and Moscelyne Larkin) attended the unveiling ceremony. This was the first time they had been together in one place. Working from several photographs of each dancer, Larsen created a monumental piece in which, he says, "I tried for representations of how the dancers moved and appeared rather than photographic likenesses of them."[8]

While the five ballerinas commemorated in Mike Larsen's mural represent their mastery of classical and modern ballet, the Osage have maintained their tradition of ceremonial dancing. Each year, the "I'N-Lon-Schka" dances are held to choose a boy as tribal drumkeeper. The youngster who has been chosen and members of his village travel to other Osage villages where participants dance, eat, and re-establish contact with each other. Male dancers dress in silk shirts and leggings and wear imitations of the traditional "roach" hairstyle. Women wear shawls about their shoulders. Gifts are exchanged among the dancers and spectators and, at the end of the third weekend, the boy who has been chosen officially becomes the tribal drumkeeper. Many of the ceremonial dances have remained unchanged from the time when Maria Tallchief's grandmother Eliza Bigheart watched them as a child.

Tallchief received the Leadership for Freedom award of the Chicago's Roosevelt University Scholarship Association in 1986 and has been elected a member of the prestigious National Society of Arts and Letters. Henry D. Paschen retired as Chairman of the Board, Treasurer, and Director from the family construction company in 1992.

Maria Tallchief has continued her teaching into the mid-1990s and has been instrumental in making sure that the Balanchine traditions she learned are not forgotten. In 1996, she coached students at New York City's School of American Ballet on some of her greatest roles. Using notes she took when she was learning the role of the fairy in Balanchine's 1946 version of *Baiser de la Fée* (Kiss of the Fairy) to refresh her memory, she was still able at seventy-one years old, to demonstrate the steps, gestures, and facial expressions that made the role her own. The classes were also videotaped, so future dancers will be able to profit from Tallchief's teaching, as well.

Maria Tallchief has expressed her fierce determination to bring what she has learned to new generations of dancers. She has spoken of the "magic" of George Balanchine's works that she wants to carry into the future:

> My whole life really is a result of my training with Balanchine and everything he ever taught me, not only about dancing but about life, is so important to me. And I just feel the magic of Balanchine has to be maintained and if it's not, then his ballets will be gone.[9]

❖Kennedy Center Honors❖

In December 1996 Maria Tallchief joined four other American artists in receiving the nineteenth annual Kennedy Center Honors in Washington, D.C., as part of a nationally-televised ceremony. The seventy-one-year-old Tallchief looked at her award in her typical manner—as an encouragement to American dancers

— ◈ —

Maria Tallchief combined exotic looks, a noble attitude, and sometimes hidden passion with a dance technique that some critics described as "perfect" to create a complex, dramatic stage presentation. This photograph shows both the regal and passionate sides of her dancing presence.

at the beginning of their careers. Said Tallchief, "I hope it will set a precedent for young American ballerinas. You don't have to be from Russia."[10]

❖An Autobiography❖

Maria Tallchief still has at least one more project to complete in an already-crowded life. She wrote in August 1995, "At the moment I am involved with my own autobiography [written with Larry Kaplan]."[11] Her story is an inspiring one, taking her as it does from a small town among the Osage in Oklahoma to ballet stages around the world and to teaching studios and ballet company boardrooms in Chicago. Tallchief's own version of that story should be well worth reading.

From her early childhood years among the Osage people on the Oklahoma reservation, Maria Tallchief rose to fame as one of the greatest ballerinas of her time. Her life is an inspiration to young people everywhere, especially Native Americans who can look to her as a cultural role model.

Chronology

1925 ◈ Maria Tallchief is born on the Osage reservation in Fairfax, Oklahoma, and is given the name Elizabeth (Betty) Marie Tall Chief.

1933 ◈ Family moves to Los Angeles. She studies ballet there.

1940 ◈ Makes her first professional appearance at the Hollywood Bowl in Los Angeles.

1942 ◈ Joins the Ballet Russe de Monte Carlo and changes her name to Maria Tallchief.

1946 ◈ George Balanchine starts to train her and marries her.

1947 ◈ Joins the New York City Ballet (then known as the Ballet Society).

1949 ◈ Reaches a high point in her career with her starring role in Balanchine's *The Firebird*.

1950 ◈ Marriage to George Balanchine ends. Continues to perform new choreography by him for another decade.

1952 ◈ Marries Elmourza Natirboff. Ends in divorce in 1954.

1956 ◈ Marries Henry C. Paschen, Jr., a construction company executive.

1959 ◈ Gives birth to their only child, daughter Elise.

1966 ◈ Retires as a ballet dancer, continues to teach.

1973 –79 ◈ Leads Chicago's Lyric Opera Ballet and its school.

1980 –87 ◈ Serves as artistic director of the Chicago City Ballet.

1996 ◈ Is honored for lifetime achievement at the Kennedy Center Honors in Washington, D.C.

1997 ◈ Autobiography, *Maria Tallchief: America's Prima Ballerina* comes out.

CHAPTER NOTES

Chapter 1

1. Francis Mason, *Remembering Balanchine: Recollections of the Ballet Master by Those Who Knew Him* (New York: Doubleday, 1991), p. 234.

2. Richard Buckle and John Taras, *George Balanchine: Ballet Master* (New York: Random House, 1988), p. 181.

3. Adèle de Leeuw, *Maria Tallchief: American Ballerina* (Champaign, Ill.: Garrard Publishing Company, 1971), p. 125.

4. Mason, p. 233.

5. Olga Maynard, *Bird of Fire: The Story of Maria Tallchief* (New York: Dodd, Mead & Company, 1961), p. 145.

Chapter 2

1. Terry P. Wilson, *The Osage* (New York: Chelsea House Publishers, 1988), p. 13.

2. Ibid.

3. John Joseph Mathews, *The Osages: Children of the Middle Waters* (Norman, Okla.: University of Oklahoma Press, 1961), pp. 23–24.

4. Terry P. Wilson, *The Underground Reservation: Osage Oil* (Lincoln, Nebr.: University of Nebraska Press, 1985), pp. 8–9.

5. Washington Irving, ed. John Francis McDermott, *A Tour of the Prairies* (Norman, Okla.: University of Oklahoma Press, 1956), pp. 21, 44.

6. George Catlin, *Letters and Notes on the North American Indians* (New York: Clarkson N. Potter, Inc., 1975), p. 275.

7. Ibid., p. 277.

8. Matthews, p. 637.

9. Wilson, *The Undergound Reservation*, p. 11.

Chapter 3

1. William K. Powers, *Indians of the Southern Plains* (New York: G.P. Putnam's Sons, 1971), p. 44.

2. Terry P. Wilson, *The Osage* (New York: Chelsea House Publishers, 1988), pp. 77–79.

3. *Handbook of Labor Statistics* (Washington, D.C.: U.S. Department of Labor Bureau of Labor Statistics, 1966), p. 475.

4. "Talented Tallchief: We Find Our Own Ballerina," *Newsweek*, October 11, 1954, p. 105.

5. Pigeon Crowle, *Enter the Ballerina* (London: Faber and Faber Limited, 1955), p. 139.

6. Lewis Burke Frumkes, *The Logophile's Orgy: Favorite Words of Famous People* (New York: Delacorte Press, 1995), p. 189.

Chapter 4

1. Olga Maynard, *Bird of Fire: The Story of Maria Tallchief* (New York: Dodd, Mead & Co., 1961), p. 10.

2. Ibid., p. 16.

3. Pigeon Crowle, *Enter the Ballerina* (London: Faber and Faber Limited, 1955), p. 142.

4. Maynard, pp. 10–11.

5. Elisabeth P. Myers, *Maria Tallchief: America's Prima Ballerina* (New York: Grosset & Dunlap, 1966), p. 37.

6. "Maria Tallchief Dance Magazine 1960 Winner," *Dance Magazine*, April, 1961, p. 33.

7. Marion E. Gridley, *Maria Tallchief: The Story of an American Indian* (Minneapolis, Minn.: Dillon Press, Inc., 1973), p. 22.

8. Crowle, p. 143.

Chapter 5

1. Olga Maynard, *Bird of Fire: The Story of Maria Tallchief* (New York: Dodd, Mead & Co., 1961), p. 26.
2. Ibid., p. 22.
3. Marion E. Gridley, *Maria Tallchief: The Story of an American Indian* (Minneapolis, Minn.: Dillon Press, Inc., 1973), p. 30.
4. Elisabeth P. Myers, Maria Tallchief: *America's Prima Ballerina* (New York: Grosset & Dunlap, 1966), pp. 63–64, 66.
5. Maynard, p. 31.
6. Ibid., p. 64.
7. Ibid., p. 66.

Chapter 6

1. Bernard Taper, *Balanchine: A Biography* (New York: Times Books, 1984), p. 31.
2. Richard Buckle and John Taras, *George Balanchine: Ballet Master* (New York: Random House, 1988), p. 7.
3. Ibid., p. 10.
4. Ibid., p. 15.
5. Taper, p. 98.
6. Ibid.
7. Buckle and Taras, p. 51.
8. Switzer, p. 198.
9. Ibid., p. 133.
10. Ibid., p. 77.
11. Walter Terry, *The Ballet Companion: A Popular Guide for the Ballet-Goer* (New York: Dodd, Mead & Company, 1968), p. 46.
12. Robert Coe, *Dance in America* (New York: E.P. Dutton, 1985), p. 56.
13. Ibid., p. 46.
14. George Balanchine, ed. Francis Mason, *Balanchine's New Complete Stories of the Great Ballets* (Garden City, N.Y.: Doubleday & Company, Inc., 1968), pp. 429–430.

15. "Kennedy Center Honors," CBS–TV, December 27, 1996.

Chapter 7

1. Robert Tracy, *Balanchine's Ballerinas: Conversations With the Muses* (New York: Linden Press/Simon & Schuster, 1983), p. 104.

2. Olga Maynard, *Bird of Fire: The Story of Maria Tallchief* (New York: Dodd, Mead & Company, 1961), p. 83.

3. Ibid.

4. Ibid., p. 95–96.

5. Ibid., p. 87.

6. Ibid.

7. Camille Hardy, "Chicago's Soaring City Ballet," *Dance Magazine*, April 1982, p. 73.

8. Maynard, p. 133.

9. Marion E. Gridley, *Maria Tallchief: The Story of an American Indian* (Minneapolis, Minn.: Dillon Press, Inc., 1973), p. 53.

10. Doris Hering, "The Season in Review . . . ," *Dance Magazine*, January 1950, p. 12.

11. "Brilliant Bird," *Newsweek,* December 19, 1949, p. 75.

12. Pigeon Crowle, *Enter the Ballerina* (London: Faber and Faber Limited, 1955), p. 147.

13. Walter Terry, *The Dance in America* (New York: Harper & Brothers Publishers, 1956), p. 182.

14. Edwin Denby, eds. Robert Cornfield and William MacKay, *Dance Writings* (New York: Alfred A. Knopf, 1986), p. 388.

15. Ibid., p. 426.

16. Walter Terry, *I Was There: Selected Dance Reviews and Articles 1936–1976* (New York: Marcel Dekker, Inc., 1978), p. 491.

Chapter 8

1. Olga Maynard, *Bird of Fire: The Story of Maria Tallchief* (New York: Dodd, Mead & Company, 1961), p. 157.

2. Francis Mason, *I Remember Balanchine: Recollections of the Ballet Master by Those Who Knew Him* (New York: Doubleday, 1991), p. 242.

3. John Gruen, "Tallchief and the Chicago City Ballet," *Dance Magazine*, December, 1984, p. HC–25.

4. Richard Buckle and John Taras, *George Balanchine, Ballet Master* (New York: Random House, 1988), pp. 185–186.

5. Ibid.

6. Ibid.

7. Gruen, p. HC–25.

8. Sarah Moore Hall, "Ex-Ballet Star Maria Tallchief Warns Her Young Students: Expect to Wait and Weep," *People Weekly*, August 13, 1979, p. 95.

9. Marion E. Gridley, *Maria Tallchief: The Story of an American Indian* (Minneapolis, Minn.: Dillon Press, Inc., 1973), p. 67.

10. Robert Tracy and Sharon DeLano, *Balanchine's Ballerinas: Conversations With the Muses* (New York: Linden Press/ Simon & Schuster, 1983), p. 105.

11. Gridley, p. 63.

12. Ibid.

13. Maynard, p. 168.

14. Walter Terry, *A Ballet Companion: A Popular Guide for the Ballet-Goer* (New York: Dodd, Mead & Company, 1968), p. 133.

15. Maynard, pp. 172–173.

16. Don McDonagh, *George Balanchine* (Boston: Twayne Publishers, 1983), p. 108.

17. Elisabeth P. Myers, *Maria Tallchief: America's Prima Ballerina* (New York: Grosset & Dunlap, 1966), p. 169.

18. Hall, p. 98.

Chapter 9

1. Felicia Henderson, "Informal Report on Oklahoma's Indian Ballerinas and Their Families," *Dance Magazine*, December 1957, p. 18.

2. Ibid.

3. Olga Maynard, *Bird of Fire: The Story of Maria Tallchief* (New York: Dodd, Mead & Co., 1961), p. 186.

4. Marion E. Gridley, *Maria Tallchief: The Story of an American Indian* (Minneapolis, Minn.: Dillon Press, Inc., 1973), p. 72.

5. "Dance Magazine's Awards Presentation," *Dance Magazine*, June 1961, p. 59.

6. Walter Terry, *I Was There: Selected Dance Reviews and Articles, 1936–1976* (New York: Marcel Dekker, Inc., 1978), p. 490.

7. Ibid., p. 489.

8. Ibid., p. 490.

9. Robert Garis, *Following Balanchine* (New Haven, Conn.: Yale University Press, 1995), p. 194.

10. Elisabeth P. Myers, *Maria Tallchief: America's Prima Ballerina* (New York: Grosset & Dunlap, 1966), p. 174.

Chapter 10

1. Sarah Moore Hall, "Ex-Ballet Star Maria Tallchief Warns Her Young Students: Expect to Wait and Weep," *People Weekly*, August 13, 1979, p. 98.

2. Camille Hardy, "Chicago's Soaring City Ballet," *Dance Magazine*, April 1982, p. 73.

3. Ibid.

4. Ibid., p. 76.

5. Hugh Boulware, "The Master: Maria Tallchief Recalls Her Years as a Prodigy of Balanchine," *Chicago Tribune*, November 23, 1989, p. 5:3:2.

6. Ibid.

7. Jennifer Allen, "Cottages by the Sea: Maria Tallchief and Henry D. Paschen on Martha's Vineyard," *Architectural Digest*, October 1987, p. 224.

8. Telephone interview with author, June 23, 1996.

9. "All Things Considered," National Public Radio, December 6, 1996.

10. Irvin Molotsky, "Five Honored at Kennedy Center Gala," *The New York Times*, December 6, 1996, p. C13.

11. Letter to author from Maria Tallchief, August 16, 1995.

⚛⇨ GLOSSARY ⇦⚛

Note on Pronunciation: Dance terms derived from foreign languages (especially French) are usually pronounced in English close to how the terms are said in the original tongue. In the pronunciation guide used below, the accented syllable is given in CAPITAL LETTERS. The following letter combinations have been used to approximate the correct pronunciation:

---

aw(n) = "aw" said through the nose (for example, premier danceur = "pruh-mee-AY daw(n)-SIR").

oo = the sound in book (for example, pas de deux = "PAH duh DOO").

oow = the sound in cool (for example, tutu = TOOW-toow).

weh(n) = "weh" said through the nose (for example, pointe = pweh(n)t).

◈ **ballerina (bal-uh-REE-nah)**—A leading female dancer in a ballet company. The star among a company's ballerinas is known as a prima (PREE-mah) ballerina.

◈ **ballet (bal-AY)**—A classical dance form or the theatrical presentation of this kind of dancing, set to musical accompaniment. The traditional steps and gestures, which require precision and grace, have evolved over several centuries and are combined into complex patterns, usually performed as solos, duets (*pas de deux*) and group movements by the *corps de ballet*.

◈ **ballet master or mistress**—Originally, the creator of a ballet (now called a choreographer); now, in the United States, the person who rehearses the dancers in the choreographer's steps and is sometimes responsible for scheduling performances and casting minor roles.

◈ *barre* **(bar)**—The horizontal wooden bar attached to the walls of a rehearsal hall at waist height. The dancers use it to support themselves as they practice steps.

◈ **choreographer (core-ee-AH-gruh-fur)**—The creator of a ballet who combines traditional dance steps, gestures and movements into a ballet or other dance performance and arranges them into artistically satisfying sequences for the dancers to perform. A choreographer's work is known as choreography (core-ee-AH-gruh-fee).

◈ *corps de ballet* **(CORE duh bal-AY)**—The dancers who support the ballerina and *premier danceur* in a ballet company. Also known as the ensemble or chorus.

◈ *divertissement* **(dee-VAIR-teess-MAW(N))**—A part of a ballet that has no connection with the plot, often including especially brilliant or difficult steps and movements. Also, sometimes, a ballet without a plot.

◈ **five positions**—The traditional positions of the feet that beginning dancers have to master, the basis of a ballet dancer's technical training.

◈ *fouetté* **(foow-eh-TAY)**—A dance movement in which the dancer spins while pivoting on the foot of one leg (alternating on and off pointe with that leg) while "whipping" the other leg in and out with a circular motion. The movement is often combined with rapid turns, *fouettés en tournant* (foow-eh-TAY aw(n) toor-NAW(N)).

❖ **jeté (jeh-TAY)**—A dancer's arc-like leap, taking off from the floor on one foot and landing on the other.

❖ **leotard (LEE-uh-tard)**—The one-piece garment covering the dancer's entire torso. Originally rehearsal clothing, leotards are often used as stage costumes in modern dances.

❖ **pas (pah)**—A dance step or movement; also, a short dance or dance passage.

❖ **pas de deux (PAH duh DOO)**—A dance duet. A *grand* (grahn) *pas de deux* is a dance for two performed by a ballerina and a *premier danceur.*

❖ **pas seul (pah SOOL)**—A solo dance, also known as a variation.

❖ **pirouette (peer-oow-ETT)**—A complete turn of a body performed on one leg, with the point of the foot of the other leg at the kneecap of the first leg.

❖ **plié (plee-AY)**—A bending of the knees while keeping the feet turned out in one of the five positions.

❖ **pointe (pweh(n)t)**—The tip of the toe. A female ballet dancer who moves on the tips of her toes, wearing blocked toe slippers for extra support, is said to be dancing "on pointe."

❖ **port de bras (PORE duh BRAH)**—The positions and movements of a ballet dancer's arms.

❖ **premier danceur (pruh-mee-AY daw(n)-SIR)**—A leading male dancer in a ballet company.

❖ **tutu (TOOW-toow)**—In modern dance, the short, ruffled skirt worn by a female ballet dancer that exposes the entire leg.

❖ **variation**—A solo dance; also known as a *pas seul.*

FURTHER READING

BOOKS

Life and Career of Maria Tallchief

De Leeuw, Adele. *Maria Tallchief: American Ballerina.* Champaign, Ill.: Garrard Publishing Company, 1971.

Gridley, Marion E. *Maria Tallchief: The Story of an American Indian.* Minneapolis, Minn.: Dillon Press, Inc., 1973.

———. *American Indian Women.* New York: Hawthorn Books, Inc., 1974.

Livingston, Lili Cockerille. *American Indian Ballerinas.* Norman, Okla.: University of Oklahoma Press, 1997.

Maynard, Olga. *Bird of Fire: The Story of Maria Tallchief.* New York: Dodd, Mead & Co., 1961.

Myers, Elisabeth P. *Maria Tallchief: America's Prima Ballerina.* New York: Grosset & Dunlap, 1966.

Tallchief, Maria with Larry Kaplan. *Maria Tallchief: America's Prima Ballerina.* New York: Henry Holt & Company, Inc., 1997.

Tracy, Robert. *Balanchine's Ballerinas: Conversations with the Muses.* New York: Linden Press/Simon & Schuster, 1983.

Twentieth Century Ballet and George Balanchine

Anderson, Jack. *Ballet and Modern Dance: A Concise History.* Princeton, N.J.: Princeton Book Company, Publishers, 1986.

Au, Susan. *Ballet and Modern Dance.* New York: Thames and Hudson, 1988.

Balanchine, George. ed. Francis Mason. *George Balanchine's Complete Stories of the Great Ballets.* Garden City, N.Y.: Doubleday & Co., Inc., 1964.

Buckle, Richard and John Taras. *George Balanchine: Ballet Master.* New York: Random House, 1988.

Chujoy, Anatole. *The New York City Ballet.* New York: Alfred A. Knopf, 1953.

———— and P. W. Manchester. *The Dance Encyclopedia (rev.).* New York: Simon and Schuster, 1967.

Clarke, Mary and Clement Crisp. *The Ballet Goer's Guide.* New York: Alfred A. Knopf, 1981.

———— and David Vaughan. eds. *The Encyclopedia of Dance and Ballet.* New York: G.P. Putnam's Sons, 1977.

Coe, Robert. *Dance in America.* New York: E.P. Dutton, 1985.

Denby, Edwin. *Looking at Dance.* New York: Horizon Press, 1968.

Kirstein, Lincoln. *Thirty Years: Lincoln Kirstein's New York City Ballet (rev.).* New York: Alfred A. Knopf, 1978.

Mason, Francis. *I Remember Balanchine: Recollections of the Ballet Master by Those Who Knew Him.* New York: Doubleday, 1991.

McDonagh, Don. *George Balanchine.* Boston: Twayne Publishers, 1983.

Taper, Bernard. *Balanchine: A Biography.* New York: Times Book, 1984.

Terry, Walter. *The Ballet Companion: A Popular Guide for the Ballet-Goer.* New York: Dodd, Mead & Company, 1968.

————. *I Was There: Selected Dance Reviews and Articles 1936–1976.* New York: Audience Arts/Marcel Dekker, Inc., 1978.

Wilson, G.B.L. *Dictionary of Ballet (rev.).* New York: Barnes & Noble, Inc., 1961.

Oklahoma/The Osage

Catlin, George ed. Michael M. Mooney. *Letters and Notes on the North American Indians*. New York: Clarkson N. Potter, Inc., 1975.

Glasscock, C.B. *Then Came Oil: The Story of the Last Frontier.* New York: The Bobbs-Merrill Company, 1938.

Irving, Washington. *A Tour on the Prairies* ed. John Francis McDermott. Norman, Okla.: University of Oklahoma Press, 1956.

Mathews, John Joseph. *The Osages: Children of the Middle Waters.* Norman, Okla.: University of Oklahoma Press, 1961.

McReynolds, Edwin. Oklahoma: *A History of the Sooner State.* Norman, Okla.: University of Oklahoma Press, 1964.

Wilson, Terry P. *The Osage.* New York: Chelsea House Publishers, 1988.

——— *The Underground Reservation: Osage Oil*. Lincoln, Nebr.: University of Nebraska Press, 1985.

MAGAZINE AND NEWSPAPER ARTICLES

Allen, Jennifer. "Cottage by the Sea: Maria Tallchief and Henry D. Paschen on Martha's Vineyard." *Architectural Digest.* October 1987, p. 171.

"American as Wampum." *Time.* February 26, 1951, pp. 76–77.

Boulware, Hugh. "The Master: Maria Tallchief Recalls Her Years as a Prodigy of Balanchine." *Chicago Tribune.* November 23, 1989, p. 5:3.

"Brilliant Bird." *Newsweek.* December 19, 1949, p. 75.

Croce, Arlene. "All-American." *The New Yorker.* December 9, 1996, p. 80.

"Dance Magazine's Awards Presentation." *Dance Magazine.* June 1961, p. 30.

Gruen, John. "Tallchief and the Chicago City Ballet." *Dance Magazine,* December 1984, p. HC-25.

Hall, Sarah Moore. "Ex-Ballet Star Maria Tallchief Warns Her Young Students: Expect to Wait and Weep." *People Weekly.* August 13, 1979, pp. 95–96, 98.

Hardy, Camille. "Chicago's Soaring City Ballet." *Dance Magazine.* April 1982, pp. 71–76.

Henderson, Felicia. "Informal Report on Oklahoma's Indian Ballerinas and Their Families." *Dance Magazine.* December 1957, p. 17.

Hering, Doris. "Re-Enter—The Ballet Russe de Monte Carlo." *Dance Magazine.* October 1954, pp. 12–17.

"Maria Tallchief Dance Magazine 1960 Winner." *Dance Magazine.* April 1961, p. 33.

"More Athletic, Less Poetic." *Time.* July 24, 1950, p. 48.

Reginato, James. "Intermezzo in Manhattan: The Pied-à-Terre of Maria Tallchief and Henry D. Paschen." *Architectural Digest.* July 1988, p. 85.

Smith, Wes. "Troupe Puts Best Foot Forward: Abandoned Ballet Dancers Vow to Remain Together." *Chicago Tribune.* November 12, 1987, pp. 3:1, 24.

Solway, Diane. "In a Dancer's World, the Inexorable Foe Is Time." *The New York Times.* June 8, 1986, p. 2:1, 24.

Terry, Walter. "Maria Tallchief and the Maryinsky Tradition." *Theatre Arts.* September 1961, pp. 57–59, 70.

☞ INDEX ☜